MW00711895

Leaning
Towards Pisa

Leaning Towards Pisa

AN ITALIAN LOVE STORY

SUE HOWARD

BANTAM
SYDNEY AUCKLAND TORONTO NEW YORK LONDON

To protect the identities of those involved, some names of people and places have been changed.

LEANING TOWARDS PISA
A BANTAM BOOK

First published in Australia and New Zealand in 2005
by Bantam

Copyright © Sue Howard, 2005

All rights reserved. No part of this publication may be reproduced,
stored in a retrieval system, transmitted in any form or by any means,
electronic, mechanical, photocopying, recording or otherwise, without
the prior written permission of the publisher.

National Library of Australia
Cataloguing-in-Publication Entry

    Howard, Sue (Susan Kathleen).
    Leaning towards Pisa.

    ISBN 1 86325 519 2.

    1. Howard, Sue (Susan Kathleen). 2. Pisa (Italy) - Social
    life and customs. I. Title.

945.55

Transworld Publishers,
a division of Random House Australia Pty Ltd
20 Alfred Street, Milsons Point, NSW 2061
http://www.randomhouse.com.au

Random House New Zealand Limited
18 Poland Road, Glenfield, Auckland

Transworld Publishers,
a division of The Random House Group Ltd
61–63 Uxbridge Road, Ealing, London W5 5SA

Random House Inc
1745 Broadway, New York, New York 10036

Text designed and typeset by Midland Typesetters, Maryborough, Victoria
Printed and bound by Griffin Press, Netley, South Australia

10 9 8 7 6 5 4 3 2 1

This book is dedicated to Dee and
Andrew Hilton – *amici del cuore*

'Nobody with a dream should come to Italy. No matter how dead and buried the dream is thought to be, in Italy it will rise and walk again.'
Elizabeth Spencer, *The Light in the Piazza*

'Gravitation cannot be held responsible for people falling in love.'
Albert Einstein

Contents

CHAPTER 1

At home in Sydney, 1999

Very early one sultry February morning – at 2.30 am to be precise – I started into unexpected consciousness. I'd been stabbed! Someone had thrust a knife deep into my right-hand side. I could feel it slicing through my flesh. The pain was excruciating. I ran my hand down my body. There were no signs of injury.

I got out of bed, staggered across the soft, deep-pile wool carpet and stumbled into the bathroom. I switched on the lights over the handbasin and looked at my reflection in the mirror. I'd turned a pale, not unattractive shade of yellow. Shaking with shock and pain, I sat on the loo and peed rusty brown water. I knew I was in big trouble.

Don't panic, don't panic, I told myself. This sort of thing happens all the time. Then why had I never heard of it? Don't panic! Call someone.

Who? Mentally I ran through the list, beginning with my friend Jane. And wake her household? Not at this hour.

My father? He was now nearly eighty, and he and his third wife, Françoise, lived an hour away on the other side of Sydney. He would panic more than me.

My weekend boyfriend? Paul lived over the other side of town, too. Besides, it wasn't the weekend.

My daughter, Sam, in Ireland? She was now a qualified nurse, so she could advise me. But she also had a new baby. I didn't want to scare her.

My son, Matthew, and Rachel, the lovely young woman he'd married and settled down with in New Zealand? It was 5 am their time. What could they do?

Hand trembling, I reached for the phone and rang my doctor's emergency number. They put me straight through to a smooth-voiced locum. 'Go to the nearest hospital immediately,' he said. 'If you can't get a taxi, call an ambulance. Immediately.'

I didn't like the way he repeated himself.

'You have a blocked bile duct,' the doctor at the hospital told me. 'We have to operate immediately.' There was that word again.

The nurse, a friendly young man clearly used to putting people at their ease, gave me an injection 'to take the edge off it' and said he'd be back for me in a few minutes. I lay on the trolley and felt myself floating off. I'm sure most people start thinking about their nearest and dearest in such moments. I found myself back in the picture postcard village on the outskirts of Cambridge where I'd been living eight years earlier. My two children had recently left home: Sam to train as a nurse in London and Matthew to travel. I had a job in publishing that I liked, a good salary, a range of friends and lived in an interesting part of England. If there was a down-side, it was the lack of a nice man in my life and the fact that, even though I'd lived in Cambridge for ten years, I hated the cold winters. Life is never perfect, I told myself.

I'd become a mother at eighteen and a single mother eight years later when my marriage broke up. At the time we were living near Sydney. With Sam at school and Matthew at kindergarten, I had enrolled at university to do a degree in English. The sense of confidence I gained from studying, learning and being my own person was one of the major elements in my marriage break-up. But then we'd married so young – my husband was still studying geology at university in London, and I'd just escaped from boarding school, already pregnant – the odds were firmly against us from the start.

Being such a young mother, all my adult life had been formed round my children. I'd looked forward to the day when I'd have more freedom: but when the time came, I somehow felt lost. I threw myself into my work – and then later the same year – 1990 – the publishing company I was working for folded and I lost my job. 'Life begins at forty', the saying goes. I had just turned forty and it felt like my life was unravelling. With nothing more to lose, I went along to a workshop entitled 'What to Do with Your Life'. Perhaps it would spark some ideas.

The workshop leader, who introduced herself as Carole, smiled and then focused on the group.

If you don't know what you do want in life, she began, you'll get a lot of what you don't want. Her voice was clear and firm with a slight American accent. I winced. I'd always been a bit cynical about what I considered American evangelising self-help programs, but I was wrong. It was a challenging, fun day. In the final session we each had to report back to the group what we'd discovered about ourselves, and outline one thing that we were going to do in the immediate future, and another before we died.

When it was my turn, I told the group: 'In the immediate future, I'm going to go back to Australia to develop a life of my own and spend some time with my father. And before I die, I'm going to live and work in another culture, one where they don't speak English.'

Well, I'd achieved my first resolution, and here I was eight years later on a surgical trolley in a Sydney hospital to prove it. Through the haze of the pre-med I could still hear Carole's voice: 'Don't waste your life . . . Things happen for a reason . . . Pay attention and don't fall asleep on the job . . .' I was thinking about not falling asleep on the job when I finally lapsed into unconsciousness.

The surgeon found more than fifty smooth, little white stones which he presented to me in a small clear plastic container with a yellow lid.

I was still groggy from the anaesthetic. 'Do I have to take these?' I asked the nurse.

'I wouldn't advise it,' she replied. 'They're your gallstones.'

I developed complications and the hospital doctor called a specialist, a dapper young man in his early forties dressed in a pinstriped shirt with gold cufflinks. He skim-read my notes and then pronounced: 'No work, total rest, no alcohol and a course of antibiotics – for two months.'

'But . . .' I said. Two months! I was sales manager for a small publishing firm which specialised in legal material. We also ran two bookshops, one in Sydney and one in Melbourne. It was similar to the work I'd been doing in Cambridge, only this time I also had a hand in managing the shops.

'But . . .' I said again. Hadn't this man ever heard of customers, sales targets, paperwork or mortgage repayments?

'You've been seriously ill,' he cut in. 'Do you want to get better or not?'

'So, let me get this straight,' I said slowly . . . and then found myself lost for words.

I went home and lay on the couch. This had all happened too quickly. I hadn't had time to come to terms with any of it, and now I didn't know where to begin.

I rang Jane. We'd been friends since university days. So much so that when I'd returned to Sydney to live on my own, I'd stayed with her and her husband, Brian. At that time, two of their four children were still at home. One month turned into two, two into three, and finally I ended up staying two years. I suppose it was an unusual arrangement. It certainly surprised people when I mentioned it. Jane was the eldest of seven, and used to waifs and strays. She and Brian lived in a large, convenient house with space for everyone, and

I was always on hand to house-sit, baby-sit or help with homework. Looking back, I realise that for me it was a period of transition: I still had the emotional comfort of a family setting, but was living my own life and beginning to gain the confidence I needed to strike out on my own.

Jane came over straight away, bringing a bag of provisions and a big bunch of flowers. She headed for the kitchen and busied herself setting out orange juice, rolls and butter, and a selection of cold meats and fruit. I watched her bustling around in mother hen mode, her thick copper hair glinting in the shafts of sun that slanted through the blinds.

She could be Irish, I thought, with her pale skin and reddish hair. But I knew she wasn't. She came from New Zealand. With five younger sisters and a brother, Jane'd been 'mothering' since she was three. No wonder she was so good at it.

'How're you feeling?' she asked, sitting beside me on the couch and giving me a big hug.

'I feel terrible,' I wailed, 'and some upper-class git has just ended my life for me!'

'What are you talking about?' Jane was used to my occasional less-than-rational outbursts.

'The specialist says I have to stay at home, take antibiotics and not touch alcohol for two whole months!'

'Good!' she said.

Good? What sort of friend was she?

'I don't mean good, you're sick. I mean good, you're going to be forced to slow down. You were very tired and run down before this all happened.'

'Was I?' I hadn't had time to notice.

'Yes. You couldn't have kept up that pace forever.' She paused, looked me in the eye (a sure sign she was being serious), and said: 'Why don't you use the time to relax and rest and think about your options? What happened to your plans to travel and write?'

I looked at her – calm, with time for everyone – and remembered how we'd talked about our visions for the future. Mine never included working sixty hours a week and living on takeaways. However, one crucial difference was that Jane had a loving husband who supported her financially – and I didn't.

Suddenly, there was a thump.

'What's that noise?' Jane asked.

From the flat upstairs came a slow scraping on the floor to the unmistakable rhythm of a bed being used for purposes other than sleeping.

'Oh,' I replied, 'that's just my neighbour's regular goat-rutting session.'

A finale worthy of Tosca throwing herself off the battlements indicated that peace was soon to come.

'It's one of the many delights of flatland living,' I continued.

'In that case,' said Jane, 'I'm pleased I live in a house with lovely thick double brickwork. But while we're on the subject, how's Paul? Has he upped the ante?'

I was defensive. I knew Jane didn't think much of my romantic arrangements. 'Well, he's very busy at the moment, but he rings when he can. And in any case, it's not that sort of relationship.'

'Exactly what sort of relationship is it then?'

I didn't reply. Jane's experience of married life had been more positive than mine. She knew the value of a committed relationship, one in which the people involved created something stronger than their individual selves. My own fragmented upbringing and divorce had led me to doubt that I would ever get up the courage to have another go. Paul and I were friends – lovers as well, but mainly friends. He didn't want anything more, and neither did I. We'd met at a work function and I'd been attracted by his warmth and gentleness. We laughed at the same things, and shared a passion for films. We started seeing each other at weekends, with phone calls and the occasional coffee during the week. It was gentle and easy. Later I understood that Paul had given me something very valuable: the chance to feel safe with a man and to heal some of the emotional gashes from my past.

Jane left and as I lay there, I thought about what she'd said. I looked around my flat – the spacious sitting and dining area that I'd had painted pale yellow, the pictures, including an Eva Hannah oil painting of a Mediterranean landscape, the books that I'd bought and never read, the terrace with the Italian outdoor furniture that caught the bright, early morning sun – and thought: I've worked hard for this. Now I'm going to relax and enjoy it.

I picked up one of the paperbacks Jane had brought me and discovered that I was now unable to read. I looked at the pages but could absorb only one or two words before my thoughts veered from the book to fears and misgivings. What if I didn't get better? How would I pay the mortgage?

Part-time work? Not enough money. The vision of a Victorian poorhouse was beginning to loom in front of me. I was saved from myself by the phone ringing. It was Sam. I could hear the baby wailing in the background.

'Two months on the settee? You wouldn't like to swap, would you?' she asked. And then: 'Why don't you come over here for a while? Your granddaughter is dying to meet you.'

The next call was my father, Greek to the core: 'Two months? Let's get another opinion. There's someone I know here – an excellent man . . . Are you eating properly? Are the Greek boys looking after you?'

This was a reference to the Greek shopkeepers in the store across the road. When I'd first moved in, my father had been with me when I'd gone to buy provisions. On discovering I had a Greek father, the boys treated me like a long-lost cousin. Nothing was too much trouble. I was presented with the best fruit and vegetables and also given a discount. Greeks are like that – they stick together and help each other out.

'Yes, Dad, don't worry. Nico comes over every day.'

'Good. Well, let me know if I can do anything.'

'Yes, I will,' I said, knowing that this was just a formality.

An hour or so later, Nico did indeed arrive, carrying not only my groceries but a newspaper and my mail. 'You're looking better today,' he said.

I didn't feel better. He was probably trying to cheer me up.

Nico, a short stocky man in his late thirties, put the groceries on the table but made no move to go; he liked to hang round for a chat. That's another Greek trait – they never

9

pass up a chance to exchange a few words. I was people starved and only too pleased for a bit of human contact.

'You know,' he said, 'you look just like your dad but you don't look Greek. How do you explain that?'

'Because my mother was English,' I said.

'Was English?' he queried.

'Yes, she died when I was young.'

All the Greeks I've ever met have been curious. I'm not sure why. Perhaps it's a genetic trait.

'So,' Nico continued, 'when did your dad come to Sydney?'

'Nearly twenty years ago. He was in Greece before that. I didn't see much of him when I was growing up. It's only over the past eight years since I've been back in Sydney that we've got close.'

My mother and father had met in Athens shortly after the war, when my mother was working for the UN Relief Agency. My father, who was handsome, charming and a philanderer, probably considered an attractive English wife and a future in England a better prospect than civil war and uncertainty. For her part, my mother was swept off her feet by the warmth, generosity and humour of this Greek god, while nothing in her reserved, well-established middle-class upbringing had taught her to recognise the danger signs. They settled in London, had two babies in quick succession – my older sister and me – and separated when I was two. My father remarried twice: firstly to Marietta, the Austrian mother of my younger sister, and then to Françoise who, as the name suggests, is French. My sisters and I used to joke about it: at least, we used to say, he's cosmopolitan in his choice of women.

'That's good,' Nico interrupted my reverie. 'It's important for families to be together.'

I didn't think this was the moment to remind him about Sam in Ireland and Matthew in New Zealand. Instead, I just said: 'You know, Nico, families can be complicated.'

'Not in Greece!' he replied.

I thought of mentioning the Onassis family, but decided to let it go.

I picked up the mail and leafed through the brightly coloured flyers. I'd never had time for junk mail before. Besides, I wouldn't have been caught dead looking at where I could get cheap deodorant. Now, I looked forward to the faces of the smiling women and tanned men entreating me to buy this, that or the other. Three weeks in hospital and a further four lying on the couch were taking their toll. My brain had turned to mush and I was morphing into something unrecognisable.

In amongst the flyers was an adult education program. I glanced through it and something caught my eye. It was a four-week course at the New South Wales Art Gallery which involved studying pictures as well as learning how to describe them in both English and Italian. Knowledge of Italian, it said, was helpful but not obligatory. Perfect: I could spend an hour or so each week drifting round the art gallery and tie it in with my weekly doctor's visit. It would give me social contact and also prevent my brain from rotting.

I'd been to Italy only once, in the August I'd turned sixteen. My father's second wife, Marietta, took my little sister, Isobel, and me to Riccione on the Adriatic coast while my father was busy working in London. I'd spent occasional weekends with them in London, but this was the first time without my father and I was a little nervous. But I needn't have worried. Marietta was calm and friendly and we got on well. We stayed in a hotel overlooking the long, sandy beach, and spent our days lazing around in deckchairs or cooling off in the calm, blue-grey water. We ate multi-course lunches that lasted two hours, and managed an afternoon gelato as well. Italian ice cream, I decided, was the most heavenly thing I'd ever tasted.

Isobel, who was seven at the time and hugely sociable, befriended another family with children, so one day Marietta and I took a bus trip to the surrounding villages, just the two of us. Marietta was my first exposure to a cultured European. She was stylish and knew how to dress, and she also under-stood art and music. She explained the different architectural styles of the cool dark churches where we took refuge from the scalding heat. She told me the stories of the saints and explained that in days gone by everyone – from poor, uneducated peasants to cultured nobility – would have understood the symbols depicted in the paintings. I remember standing transfixed in front of a portrait of Mary Magdalen, the stone bottle containing the oil to anoint the feet of Jesus in her left hand, the light playing on the slight smile on her lips. I was perfectly sure she was smiling at me.

The lessons at the art gallery were held on Tuesday mornings. The other eight or so participants were all retired professional people, apart from a businessman and a woman in her forties who was buying a house in Tuscany. The teacher, Valeria – an Italian beauty in her thirties with clear blue eyes and an engaging smile – was a natural. She enthused; she radiated intelligence and humour. She came from Torino, a town in the north of Italy which had been under the domination of the Savoia dynasty, whose roots went back to French rather than Italian soil. Torino, she told us, was the perfect mix of Italian lifestyle and French architecture.

The lessons were fun. Valeria spoke slowly in Italian, and then translated for those of us who understood little. She described pictures, and asked students to prepare their own descriptions. Then we all adjourned to the cafeteria and did simple grammar and translating exercises working together in small groups, the stronger students helping the weaker ones. I bought myself a basic Italian grammar book and a dictionary, and tried to make sense of the hand-outs.

I was entranced. In my idle moments, I thought back to the declaration I'd made at the workshop in Cambridge eight years before. Was Italy, with its melodic language, abundant culture and beautiful people the country I was going to live and work in? I couldn't imagine how it would be possible.

At the final lesson we were all sitting in the café at the art gallery when Jenny, one of the women I'd become friendly with, asked: 'You wouldn't by any chance be interested in a couple of weeks in Tuscany in August?'

'Tell me more,' I said, perfectly sure that I was interested.

'Well, some of us on the course have booked a house in the hills behind Lucca – a farmhouse on three levels – for the month of August. Jean has had to drop out, so I thought you might like to take her place.'

'Thank you for the offer,' I said. 'I'll let you know.'

I spoke to my doctor. It was now June. Did he think I'd be well enough for a trip to Europe in August?

'As long as you don't do anything silly,' he told me. 'And keep off the alcohol.'

I made my decision. I would go to Italy for two weeks and then on to Ireland to see Sam and the baby. Now I had to make plans.

I checked the state of my finances (poor but not dire). I spoke to a colleague who was looking for accommodation and agreed that he should take over my flat on a casual basis. I didn't want to leave it empty, and the rent would cover at least some of the expenses. I rang Sam and said I was planning a visit, and then rang Jenny to confirm that I would take the room in the farmhouse. I made an appointment to see my boss, and finally rang Jane and told her what I'd done.

'Brilliant,' she exclaimed. 'How lovely! You get time with the baby and a holiday.'

I waited until the weekend to tell Paul. His job in financial management meant that he often worked long hours and spent chunks of time in Melbourne. When he wasn't working, he liked a simple life: reading, watching films and mooching round Sydney. Paul was, at heart, a bachelor, although he'd had one live-in relationship that had lasted seven years: 'I just could never see myself doing it,' he'd told me, 'wedding, babies . . . the full catastrophe.' Eventually his girlfriend left, leaving the two cats behind.

'I've decided to spend some time in Europe,' I said casually when he arrived at my place on Saturday afternoon. 'Ireland and Italy.'

'Oh,' he said, and paused. 'How long will you be away?'

'I'm not sure . . . up to three months.'

'Three months!'

Paul looked taken aback, but quickly checked himself. He knew we were both free to come and go as we pleased: 'Well,' he said, 'three months isn't so long. You'll come back a new person.'

The next morning I went to see my boss. I was going to ask for leave without pay, but as the lift door slid open onto the reception area revealing the familiar ringing telephones, secretaries rushing to and fro and people shouting down the corridor, something inside me snapped. Again I could hear that voice from the past with its slight American twang saying firmly: 'This is not a dress rehearsal!' In that moment I knew – absolutely knew – that I couldn't go back. So instead of asking for leave of absence, I resigned.

Although I realised I'd lost both the appetite and stamina for my work, not everyone saw it like that.

My father: 'You've done what? Given up your job for a holiday! Have you gone mad?' But others were more encouraging.

Matthew: 'Great, Mum. Don't worry. You'll always be able to find another job.'

Sam: 'Wonderful, you can spend longer with us.'

And the general opinion of my colleagues and friends: 'Lucky you! Wish we could bail out for a while.'

I felt nothing but relief; the decision had been made.

My last Saturday with Paul was subdued. We'd been together for four years. That's a lot of weekends. I decided on a special farewell dinner. I bought fresh salmon and made a Greek salad with fat, black kalamata olives. I put a bottle of verdelho in the fridge for Paul, and thought how much more pleasant it was when we could share a bottle of wine together. Having to cut out alcohol was, perhaps, the hardest aspect of my condition.

Paul arrived casually dressed in jeans and a navy polo shirt. He stood in the doorway, his thick dark wavy hair barely under control. The odd silver thread glittered in amongst the mass, and although he was five years younger than me, I noticed that his stomach was beginning to show the signs of too many business lunches and a sedentary lifestyle.

I suddenly felt sad. 'I'll miss you,' I said.

'I'll miss you, too.'

'We can keep in touch by phone and email.'

'Yes, we won't even notice the difference,' Paul joked. But we both knew that wasn't true.

We went to bed early, and when he left the following morning, he kissed me gently on the lips and gave me one last smile before pulling the door closed behind him.

I was having Sunday lunch with my dad and Françoise. As I no longer had a car (that had gone with the job), I took the train out to just short of the Blue Mountains where they lived. As the train sped through the western suburbs of Sydney, loosening from shabby inner city factories to Federation homes with gardens and finally to the open flat plains at the foot of the mountains, I thought about my father and the decision I'd made to get to know him. It hadn't always been easy. For many years I stored up a great deal of anger towards him for the mess he'd made of the family – firstly separating from my mother, then botching things up with Marietta, and finally settling with Françoise, first in Greece and then in Australia. Although my father had been a shadowy figure in my childhood, not only did I look like him, I also had his sense of humour and a similar take on politics. But he was a Greek male, and an older generation one at that. He was loving and generous, but he was also patriarchal and had some pretty fixed views. I was a modern woman, brought up in a different culture and without his influence. Over the years we'd had some heated discussions, but we'd also become friends.

He was waiting for me at the railway station. He'd obviously been stewing things over.

'I know you haven't been well,' he said. 'And of course you want to spend time in Ireland with the baby. You're the grandmother, after all. But why did you have to go and resign? Couldn't you do both? How are you going to survive?'

Françoise, who was closer in age to me than him and usually kept out of the firing line, said: 'Leave the poor girl alone. She's only just got here.'

But I knew he wouldn't leave it alone, in the same way

17

I knew I had no explanation that would satisfy him. So I said: 'Look, I just feel that it's the right thing to do.'

'And Paul? What does he think?'

Again, I knew that my love life wasn't what a Greek father would want for his daughter. 'Well, things between us will either continue or they won't.'

'What sort of answer is that?' He looked genuinely bewildered.

When I left he gave me a big bear hug – the type he used to give me as a child – and said: 'See you soon.'

CHAPTER 2

My first view of Pisa

The farmhouse where we were staying was in the country-side thirty minutes by car north of Lucca, which in turn was thirty minutes north of the nearest airport at Pisa. I planned to take a bus from Pisa to Lucca and then a taxi to the farmhouse. However, my connecting flight from Rome was delayed and I finally reached Pisa at one in the morning. As I stepped from the small plane into the warm night air, I felt a surge of excitement. I was here! But my enthusiasm waned slightly when I realised that everything at Pisa airport was closed. The trains and buses had stopped for the night, and the taxi rank was deserted. I had been expected at the farmhouse during the afternoon, and had rung to say that I'd be a day late. In the meantime, I'd intended to find a cheap hotel for the night. Instead, I would have to spend my first night in Italy at the airport.

I walked the length of the building, which wasn't far, but I couldn't see anywhere suitable to sleep. I noticed some stairs, climbed to the upper level, and found some inviting padded benches. I settled down, using my handbag as a pillow and putting my suitcase safely under the bench.

I had just started to doze off when someone nudged me. I opened my eyes and looked straight into the narrow brown eyes of a man wearing overalls and holding a broom: *'Non si puo', Signora, non si puo'. Stiamo chiudendo!'*

What was he saying? I had no idea, but the shaking of the head and the pulling at my sleeve told me that I wasn't going to get a good night's sleep – nor any sort of sleep – here.

'Hotel?' I asked. 'Is there a hotel near here – a modest hotel?'

'Ah,' he said, *'hotel modesto! Va bene. Le chiamo un taxi!'*

'Yes, yes, *hotel modesto* and *taxi'.* And then I added: *'Grazie.'*

'Venga,' he said, *'venga pure.'* He smiled and insisted on carrying my suitcase for me back down to the lower floor, where he rang for a taxi on his mobile phone. When the taxi driver appeared, he spoke to him rapidly in Italian. The taxi driver opened the car door for me while the other man put my suitcase in the boot, and all the while they both smiled and nodded. Italian men, I later found out, like playing gallant knights to damsels in distress, as long as the damsels aren't hideous or over eighty years old.

Five minutes later, the taxi arrived outside the main door of the two-star *hotel modesto*. The taxi driver rang the bell and jabbered away to the night porter.

The taxi driver refused to take any money from me: 'No, no,' he said, *'va bene così* [that's fine as it is].' I was touched. He really was a gentleman.

The night porter thrust some forms at me and told me that he needed my *passaporto*. In Italy, the land of lovers and secret trysts, everyone staying at a hotel has to provide a legally-recognised form of identification. Good grief, I thought, if they had this one going in Australia or England, think of the scandals. In these days of chequebook journalism, how could you ever be sure that the porter wouldn't drop a little word here or there in return for a few pieces of silver? But Italians, as I was to discover, wouldn't dream of being indiscreet in that way.

Colazione, the porter told me, was at eight and was *inclusa nel prezzo*.

Well, at least I got that – breakfast at eight and included in the tariff.

As I looked round my whitewashed *modesto* room with laminated furniture, shabby curtains and TV with no remote control I remembered how I'd imagined my first night in Italy – rustic farmhouse, cypress trees, warm summer smells . . . This wasn't it.

I lay in bed and recalled the past two days – Jane and Brian's warm and encouraging farewell from Sydney, my dad's last minute phone call: 'Keep in touch – don't forget us', and then thought about the holiday that awaited me. Tomorrow I would have a quick look round Pisa before catching the afternoon bus to Lucca and then a taxi to the farmhouse.

The noise in Italy wakes you early, and I'm not talking about the gentle hum of traffic or the chirping birds. I am talking about serious, industrial-strength, health-destroying

21

Italian noise. It started before 6 am with an accelerating roar like a jumbo jet revving up for take-off. Then followed a full five minutes of metallic clanging and clashing that was so loud I wondered if the hotel was next to a scrap metal yard. A quick glance through the window revealed a row of huge grey metal containers, and a mechanised truck which was picking up each one in turn, up-ending it, and then banging it down again on the pavement. What was this? A recycling plant?

I got back into bed, snuggled under the covers, and waited for sleep to overtake me. I ignored the first hrrrrmp, crash, bang and further hrrrrmp. It was, I imagined, the hotel opening the shutters for the day. When it happened for the fourth time, I gave up. No wonder Mediterraneans have the reputation for being excitable and quick-tempered, I thought. They're all sleep deprived.

The day was beautiful – clear and bright, and still cool. I wanted to do my looking around before the full summer heat hit at midday. The day porter gave me a photocopied map of the city and marked the hotel with a big X. He explained that it would take about twenty minutes to walk to the site of the Leaning Tower. Pisa, I discovered, is a compact town surrounded by medieval walls with arched gateways. It never takes more than twenty minutes to walk anywhere within the old city boundaries.

Breakfast was served in an airless room behind the reception desk, although the fare on offer hardly merited the word 'breakfast'. It consisted of one sad-looking slice of sponge cake wrapped in cellophane, accompanied by a pot of coffee.

Even in the dingy light of the dining room the cake was an alarmingly bright yellow and I wondered what substances had contributed to its almost luminescent glow. Not, I felt sure, plain and simple egg yolk. However, hunger got the better of me. I unwrapped the packet, dunked the cake in the rich, scalding-hot coffee and took a bite. There was a hint of almonds, followed by a sensation like having a mouthful of hot sand. I swallowed, and then gave up, concluding that the fact I was the only person at breakfast probably served as a warning.

I set off past the railway station towards a little piazza dominated by an enormous statue in the centre. The plaque read:

VITTORIO EMANUELE II *'PADRE DELLA PATRIA'*
RE D'ITALIA 1849–1878

'Father of the Homeland, King of Italy', I translated, marvelling that the little Latin I'd learned at school all those years ago had finally come in useful. The first king of a united Italy was mounted on a horse, right arm extended in a gesture of welcome, eyes turned heavenwards. His helmet and out-stretched arm were lightly caked in chalky bird droppings. He could, I thought, do with a good hosing down.

I walked on and up the narrow stone street, Corso Italia, Pisa's main shopping area. Both sides of the street were given over to small shops, mainly selling fashion, shoes and hand-bags, each shop window carefully and tastefully arranged to attract the attention of the passing throng. I knew, of course, that Italians have a reputation for being elegant and well-dressed, but nothing had prepared me for the level of swish and style I saw as I walked around this old university town. The women, although not necessarily beautiful, made the best of themselves: a colourful scarf casually thrown round the neck, a sleek handbag slung over the shoulder, or thick hair twisted up into a chic knot with a glittering comb. This elegance was particularly noticeable in older women, who seemed to take as much delight in sashaying along attracting the attention of passers-by as their much younger sisters. I thought back to my Italian holiday years ago. Perhaps I'd been too young to notice such things.

After five minutes, Corso Italia widened and I arrived at the River Arno, the khaki-coloured soup which flows through Florence and Pisa before bending and winding its way out into the Tirrenian Sea to the west. I stopped on the bridge that connects the two halves of the town. Downriver, directly on the riverbank, was a Gothic fairytale church made of white marble. With its twisted columns and delicate spires, it looked like a massively big, iced wedding cake. As far as I could see into the distance, the river was fronted by majestic four and five-storey buildings, all painted the same tones of ochre and sand. The arched wooden front doors were huge – at least six metres high – and seemed very old. Were these houses, I wondered, once inhabited by medieval giants? Behind me were the purplish mountains that give Pisa that special quality of nestling between the mountains and the sea. I took a deep breath while looking around me. 'What an amazing place!' I was talking to myself, but it hardly mattered.

I crossed the river, continued up Borgo Stretto and then turned left towards the Piazza dei Miracoli which is the site of the cathedral, baptistery and Leaning Tower. I found myself in the medieval quarter, with tall, narrow stone houses butted up against each other, and alleyways or bridges running between them – all higgledy-piggledy. One of the alleyways widened out into a square with shops under the columned porticos, and an open-air market in the centre. I stopped to look at the shops. In the *salumeria* the hanging legs of ham and salamis formed a fatty curtain between the shopkeeper and his customers. Ouside the fishmongers, which gave off a strong, sour smell in the summer heat, I spotted a large glass tank. In it was a squirming, writhing mass of live eels. And then the horse butcher. Horse? Did they eat horse in Italy as well as France? Evidently they did.

I bought some peaches from an axe-faced woman with black hair and sat in the square to eat one. Pisa seemed so alive – so bustling with life and activity – and yet so steeped in history. It reminded me of Cambridge. It had the same charm, but with the added elements of warmth, noise and chaos.

A further five minutes walk, through Piazza Dante towards Via Roma, and then suddenly I saw it, above the rusty orange roofs of the buildings, a flag fluttering from its angled top: the Leaning Tower. It is stunning – despite the lean – for its symmetry and style, which is simple yet pleasing. But for me, the true beauty is in the combined effect of the cathedral, baptistery and tower set together in a field of lush green lawn.

I sat on the marble surrounds of the cathedral and drank it

all in. I thought of the imagination, skill and talent of the people who had designed and constructed these wonders nearly a thousand years ago and felt strangely overawed: I was once again a transfixed fifteen-year-old schoolgirl in front of a painted smile in a dark church in a forgotten village on a similarly hot Italian August day.

It was time to go. I was hungry and had just enough time for lunch before collecting my suitcase and catching the bus to Lucca. Tantalising cooking aromas were coming from a nearby alley and I ventured in to investigate. I found a doorway, but still wasn't sure what sort of place it was. A man behind the counter beckoned me in, and pointed to the black oven plate where some kind of pancakes were slowly bubbling. What the hell, I thought. Whatever it was, it certainly wasn't eel or horsemeat. I held up a finger: *'Uno, per favore.'*

I watched while the man flipped the pancake onto a sheet of greaseproof paper, sprinkled it with salt, and gave it to me in an open cardboard box. I retraced my steps through the market and found a shady bench in a small square near the bridge. The pancake was scalding hot, slightly oily and had a flavour that I couldn't place. Later, I found out that it's a specialty of Pisa called *cecina*, made from a batter of mashed chickpeas and spices, fried in local olive oil.

I was running late. I walked quickly back to the bridge and had just begun to cross when a billboard caught my eye. It was leaning against the railings of a first-floor balcony surrounded by pots of bright red geraniums, ENGLISH LANGUAGE SCHOOL. I don't know if it was the magical effect of

Italy, jet lag, or just a sudden rush of blood to the head that made me turn back, walk round to the entrance of the school in the narrow lane at the back of the building, climb the dark, steep staircase to the secretary's office and leave the following message: 'I'm a qualified and experienced high school English teacher. Do you have any teaching vacancies?' I signed my name and the date, and wrote out the phone number of the holiday home. I then completely forgot about it.

My taxi pulled up at the entrance to the farmhouse just before four in the afternoon, following a remarkably simple journey. I'd collected my suitcase from the hotel and walked to the bus station, guided by yet another X marked on my map by the hotel porter. The lady in the ticket office spoke good English, and as the bus drove along the long, straight tree-lined avenue that led out of Pisa towards the mountain range that separates it from Lucca, I began once more to feel the excitement of a new adventure. The taxi rank in Lucca was next to the bus stop, and the taxi driver – a short fellow with thick black curls and hairy forearms – nodded vigorously at the address I showed him and indicated that I should get into the taxi. He turned on the radio, and we drove along listening to the strains of slow, romantic ballads interspersed with very fast Italian. All the while, the taxi driver remained mute, his expression broken only by a slow smile which increased to a grin when I paid him the eighty-thousand lire fare.

The farmhouse was set on a hill looking down towards a

deep valley covered by olive groves, vineyards and grazing land. It had its own large garden with heavy-leafed chestnut trees offering welcome shade. The house itself was built of stone with high ceilings criss-crossed with ancient wooden beams. The walls were whitewashed and every room had dark, rustic furniture.

Jenny showed me to my bedroom, which was at the top of two flights of uneven stone steps. I threw open the shutters to a rush of warm air, light and a view of terraces of silver green olive trees up into the hills beyond.

Jenny heard me gasp. 'I thought you'd like it,' she said with satisfaction. 'It's also the quietest room in the house so you can rest all you like.' She paused. 'I'll leave you to unpack. Oh . . . and dinner's at eight.'

I lay on the bed watching the light play on the vase of fresh lavender on top of the chest of drawers, then fell asleep.

When the phone call came through, I was out in the garden gazing down at the spiky cypresses and yellow farmhouses which dotted the valley. Jenny came out to get me.

'There's a call for you – it's a fellow.'

'It must be a mistake,' I said blankly, 'I haven't given anyone this number.'

'Well, he asked for you by name.'

'This,' said the educated English voice on the other end of the phone, 'is Tom Mowbray, director of the English School in Pisa. I understand you're interested in a teaching position. Could you come for an interview tomorrow afternoon – say at five?'

I was completely taken by surprise. 'Well . . . yes . . . of course,' I said.

I put the phone down. Oh no, I thought, what had I done? Was I really serious about teaching in Italy? Why did I agree to the interview – why didn't I just say sorry, there's been a misunderstanding? But after a moment's reflection, I calmed down. I didn't know anything about the school. The interview would surely be a fizzer, but it wouldn't hurt to go and have a look. It might be interesting, and – I stopped. I had a sudden flashback to the workshop in Cambridge. What had I proclaimed to the group? That I wanted to live and work in a foreign country. Well, who knows, perhaps this was going to be my chance.

The next morning, Jenny suggested we go into Lucca. She'd been to Italy many times and always hired a car so she could get around easily.

'You know, what I really love,' she told me, 'is going back to the same places time and again. You've no idea how much your perspective changes over the years.'

I liked Jenny. She was a retired teacher from Mosman, long separated from her husband, with a no-nonsense approach to life. 'He left me, you know,' she said. 'The bastard! He came home one day, packed his bag and was gone within the hour. There was another woman, of course. I was destroyed for a while – didn't think I'd make it without him.' She paused. 'It turned out to be the biggest favour he ever did me!' She let out a loud laugh. She'd obviously had more fun without her husband than with him.

Lucca is a small town surrounded by massive sixteenth

century walls which contain some of Italy's finest medieval and Renaissance architecture. There are over one hundred churches, towers and palazzi. It is also the birth place of Giacomo Puccini, composer of the operas *Madame Butterfly*, *Tosca*, *Turandot* and *La Bohème*. Jenny told me all this as we dived from one lane to the next in her hired Fiat Punto along the main road that circled the outer walls of the town, and which clearly doubled up as a Formula One racing circuit. I clung on to the dashboard, my knuckles the same shade of white as the car, while Jenny weaved in and out of the kamikaze-like traffic, apparently unfazed by driving on the right, or the reckless driving of the Italians. I didn't want to dwell on why Lucca had so many churches, but I imagined a lot of praying for safe delivery from traffic accidents had something to do with it.

What Jenny hadn't told me was that Lucca – with its narrow lanes, canals and grand squares – was like a diamond: compact, brilliant, and with flashes of colour at every turn. The main square, Piazza Napoleone, contains the elegant French style palace that Napoleon built for his sister. In the far corner of the piazza we found the *Gelateria Pinguino* which offered exquisite gelato. We strolled around the piazza licking our lemon and vanilla cones and checking out the shop windows. In July, Jenny told me, they fence off the square and stage pop concerts for two thousand people, with performers like Paul Simon, Rod Stewart and Simply Red.

'I saw Elton John here a couple of years ago,' she said.

Good grief, I thought, Jenny was over sixty, and here she was raging on till the small hours. 'Was he good?' I asked, to cover my surprise.

'Yes,' she replied. 'Brilliant!'

'You know, I'd love an evening under the Tuscan skies, raving away to music from my youth,' I said.

'But you're a *grandmother*!' Jenny replied, with an ironic laugh.

We walked into the lanes that run off the main square until we came to the Guinigi Tower. We decided the view from the top would be worth it, so we climbed – huffing and puffing – the one hundred and thirty feet. We found an ancient oak tree growing from the top and a spectacular view of the red-tiled roofs of Lucca and surrounding countryside.

By now we were both beginning to overheat, so we went to cool off in the cathedral. Churches in Italy, with their thick stone floors and walls, high roofs and few windows, offer a welcome respite from the scorching midday sun. I suddenly had a hugely irreligious thought: perhaps the hundreds of churches in this small town had more to do with taking refuge from the humid forty-degree heat than religion. I decided the cathedral wasn't the best place to express this thought, and moved on to put coins into the little machine next to Tintoretto's *The Last Supper* and watch Christ surrounded by his disciples suddenly burst into brilliant light. The painting is full of pathos, with the emotions of the characters revealed in the exquisite detail of their faces. We stared for the full two minutes until, with a little 'click', the painting was once again plunged into darkness.

We moved into a side chapel to see the tomb of Ilaria del Carretto (Hilary of the cart), the wife of Guinigi of the tower, who died in childbirth in the thirteenth century.

The sculpture of her on the tomb is extremely lifelike. John Ruskin, the English art critic, claimed that she epitomised feminine beauty. Jenny grinned and said: 'I know quite a few men who would find their women more beautiful carved in marble and stuck on a plinth.' I sensed there was quite a history behind the remark, but was too polite to ask.

It was time for lunch. We found a shaded bench in the piazza constructed on the site of a Roman amphitheatre where we sat and ate slices of takeaway pizza and drank – thankfully – glasses of ice-cold mineral water. After a stroll round the elevated city walls, which looked down over the botanic gardens and four-hundred-year-old *palazzi*, it was time to drive to Pisa, some twenty kilometres south, for my five o'clock appointment.

Tom Mowbray was a tall, thin man in his late fifties with neatly cut sparse grey hair. His tweed jacked – even in the intense heat – and neatly pressed shirt gave the impression of an archetypal English gentleman abroad. He walked with big strides, as if he were out on the moors with a shooting gun under his arm. He could, I thought, have stepped off the page of a PG Wodehouse novel.

'Let me tell you something about the school and show you round,' he said, 'and then we can get down to details.'

The school was a private language school catering for university students and business people, with a few classes for teenagers who were following the international Cambridge exams. There was also a small *bambini* class for children as young as four. He showed me the six classrooms, four of which looked over the river, and the bathroom with the toilet on a raised platform. 'I call it the throne room,' he said, and laughed.

Did he sometimes sit there with a crown on his head?, I wondered. We moved on.

There were twenty teachers – some part-time – and two secretaries. The lessons were held mainly in the evenings, starting at 6 pm and finishing at 10 pm. There was, of course, lesson preparation, marking and end-of-term exams to add to a weekly timetable of twenty-five hours classroom teaching. From what I could understand, he was describing a standard foreign-language teaching regime.

'Now,' he said, 'let's find out a bit about you.'

I handed him two scrappy pieces of paper: the résumé that I'd hastily cobbled together on the notepad that Jenny kept in the car.

'Hmm, is this it?' he asked.

'Yes,' I replied. Did he think I carried a résumé around with me on holiday?

'Good.' He smiled. 'I hate it when people arrive with pages and pages. It's such a waste of my time.'

He skim-read the two scraps. 'So,' he confirmed, 'you've got high school teaching experience. Okay. Term begins in October. Be here by the tenth. Do you have any questions?' Clearly, from his point of view the interview was drawing to a close.

And yes, I did have questions – hundreds of them. So many, in fact, that I barely knew where to begin. 'Well,' I started, 'what about accommodation?'

'You don't have to worry about that – we fix it all up for you. We've got a good information pack which outlines everything. I'll get my secretary to send one to you.'

The pay was in lire – between one and two million a month. I'd never been paid millions before. I accepted.

It was 1999 and I was forty-nine years old.

I walked out, dazed, to meet Jenny.

'So,' she said, 'how did it go?'

'He offered me a job, and I accepted.' I couldn't quite believe what I was saying.

'Good on you. But what about accommodation, visas, stuff like that?'

'I'm lucky,' I said. 'I have both British and Australian passports, so I can stay in Italy as long as I like. For the rest, apparently they sort it all out for you. They're going to send me the information. All I have to do is turn up on the tenth of October.'

There was a short silence as I began to take in the implications of what I had done. Surely this was a young person's game, but Tom Mowbray had assured me that there were other older teachers. He also didn't seem bothered by my lack of experience teaching English to foreigners ('It's personality that counts').

'Well,' I said to Jenny, 'there's a let-out clause in the contract. Either side can terminate up to six weeks into the first term. If I'm not happy, I'll leave.'

'Too right,' she replied, 'and it'll be a wonderful experience anyway.'

As she took the hairpin bends leading from the plains of

Pisa up to the mountain range around Lucca, I once again caught myself thinking, if she keeps driving like this, neither of us will have any sort of future anywhere.

That evening we celebrated with *prosecco*, the Italian sparkling wine. Jenny proposed a toast: 'As you know,' she said, 'I've been coming to Italy for years. I've seen all sorts of things happen: romances, even a death [nervous laughter], but I've never seen anyone jump ship before. Cheers!'

The rest of the holiday passed quietly. I resumed my position under the shady tree and read and thought about the strange twist that had brought me to Italy, and the even stranger twist that meant I would now be living here. As the two weeks drew to a close I was, I noticed, feeling much stronger and healthier than I had for a long time. The regime of lots of sleep, good food and company, no wine and no work, was paying off. I was also beginning to get more than a little excited at the thought of seeing, holding and cuddling my new granddaughter, Hannah, for the first time.

The flight from Pisa to London's Stansted Airport takes two hours. The flights go four times a day, and the cost – especially if you book on the Internet – can be as little as $100 return. Cheap airfares have certainly revolutionised the way people travel, I thought, as I sat with my knees up near my chin eating a soggy chicken and lettuce sandwich, looking in disbelief at the 'cup of tea' which was actually a polystyrene tumbler full to the brim with boiling water in which floated white, congealed particles of powdered milk. After a couple of seconds, something which looked horribly like a tampon rose from the depths and started seeping brown dye into the steaming scum. This liquid abomination cost me more than five dollars! Budget airlines prosper by getting you on and then ripping you off, I concluded.

I watched the Swiss Alps – their tips still covered with snow even though it was summer – pass underneath and thought about Sam and Hannah, now nearly a year old. What sort of character did she have? Would things be different with my daughter now that she was a mother herself? How would I feel when confronted by my new grandmother status?

At Stansted I changed planes for the short connecting flight to Belfast, where they were all at the airport to meet me.

Sam – who'd talked about returning to Australia when she'd finished her nursing training – chose instead to marry a Northern Irish man with deep blue eyes and thick eyelashes, and settle in the north of Ireland. I couldn't blame her – those eyes! It was also, I had to admit, partly my fault. I'd encouraged her to think for herself and be independent. When the first photos of Hannah popped up on my computer screen, I had momentary regrets. If I'd been more clingy as a mother, perhaps I'd be holding my granddaughter rather than downloading her onto my hard drive. Now here I was, holding her in my arms for the first time, this little creature with porcelain skin and – yes – deep blue eyes with thick eyelashes. I cried. We all cried – she, me and Sam. My son-in-law, Peter, looked on, bemused but smiling.

They lived in a small country town nearly an hour away

from Belfast. Peter ran a successful business and they lived in a comfortable, modern double-storey house with an oak tree in the back garden with its very own squirrel.

At dinner that evening, I announced: 'I may be spending next year a bit closer than Sydney.'

'Oh,' Sam said. I could see she was pleased. 'Where?'

'Pisa.'

Peter looked at me. 'Pisa? What will you do there?'

'Teach in a private language school – for adults, not children.'

'That's rather sudden, isn't it?'

'I suppose it is. I'll make a final decision when I see the contract.'

I quickly settled into the domestic routine that life with a young child requires. I was getting to know Hannah and enjoying the muzzy-love feeling that I now associate with being a granny. I took her for walks, pushing the stroller down the hill into the town centre. This grey market town, with its monochrome people, did nothing for me at all. Although the people individually were friendly, the place itself seemed cold and distant from the rest of the world. There wasn't a bookshop, and the nearest cinema was ten miles away. Perhaps, I thought, the Protestants and Catholics make trouble with each other because they haven't got anything else to do. It was a hugely simplistic assessment, but one that I stuck to during my connection with the north of Ireland.

One afternoon a neighbour 'came to call'. This, Sam informed me, was what people did in Northern Ireland.

I searched the recesses of my mind. Yes, I could vaguely remember visits from neighbours and polite afternoon teas: circa 1958, if my memory served me well.

A little after the appointed hour, a stout lady with a pleated skirt, gaberdine raincoat and hairstyle like the Queen arrived out of breath. She plonked herself on the settee and announced: 'Oh, I'm sorry I'm late. I'm behind today because we had visitors yesterday evening. It was a good night,' she continued. 'We had great crack.'

Crack? I looked at Sam. Was the blue-rinse on the settee, ankles bulging over the sensible lace-up shoes, a drug fiend?

'C–R–A–I–C, Mother,' Sam said slowly and carefully, as if talking to a four-year-old, 'is the word they use for fun.'

I confess to being slightly disappointed. I turned to our visitor. 'Could I offer you a cup of tea – or would you prefer something stronger?'

'Go and make the tea,' my daughter hissed at me under her breath.

True to Tom Mowbray's word, a few days after I'd arrived in Ireland, a large brown package with the insignia of the English School, Pisa, dropped onto the doormat. There was a five-page information sheet and a contract to sign and return. I asked Peter, who had experience in contracts, to check the contents.

'Well,' he concluded, 'it's pretty straightforward. It's a standard British contract. They pay your national insurance contributions, you're covered by the European Union health regulations, the contract runs from October 1999 until June

2000, and if you foul up they can sack you. I can't judge how good or bad the pay is – that will depend on the cost of living. The accommodation seems reasonable. They find private flats and negotiate fixed rents – it'll be about thirty per cent of your salary. But at the end of the day, this type of contract is more or less unenforceable: it gives guidelines but not much more.'

It sounded fine. They weren't asking me to put my head in a noose, so I signed and mailed the contract back to the school.

One day Peter came home and announced: 'We're going out tomorrow evening. My mother's going to babysit.'

I was delighted at the prospect of some deviation from our normal domestic routine. 'Oh? Where are we going?' I asked.

He grinned at me: 'Wait and see.'

I turned to Sam, who shrugged.

The following evening, dressed casually as instructed, we left the house and drove out of town.

'How far is it?' I asked Peter. I confess to having inherited the Greek trait of curiosity – I hate secrets. When someone is hiding something from me, I get agitated in my desire to know what it is. If they won't tell me, I wheedle away to see if I can get enough clues to work it out for myself.

But Peter wasn't playing my game: 'Not sure. Probably not far now.'

We were driving east (I knew that because the sun was low in the sky behind us), and heading towards the coast. But what was there on the coast: a nice restaurant? We weren't dressed for that. A boat trip? But to where? I reluctantly (very reluctantly) decided to wait and see.

After an hour of narrow, winding lanes overhung with ancient oaks and elms, we did indeed arrive at the coast and a few minutes later I saw what looked for all the world like a Loire Valley chateau appear on our left. Peter turned into the entrance and then swung into an almost full car park. The notice at the gate said KILLYLEAGH CASTLE. It was pure fairytale, with its Gothic façade, spires and crenellations. The only thing missing was Rapunzel . . . or perhaps Shrek's Princess Fiona. But I still didn't know what we were doing here. And then I saw the poster:

TONIGHT

VAN MORRISON UNDER THE STARS

And so the wish I'd made in Lucca was granted. I had my evening of raving away to the music of my youth: 'Van the Man' in black trilby and sunglasses with Georgie Fame on keyboards. It was not as I'd pictured it – under the skies in Piazza Napoleone – but in an Irish castle with the friendly, Guinness-drinking locals.

My six weeks in Ireland were drawing to a close. As I watched Sam lovingly hold her own daughter, I realised that during my stay I had taken on the role of mother of a young family once more. I had shopped, made cakes, vacuumed carpets and played with the baby. And although I had loved being a part of it, I also recognised that I wouldn't want to do it permanently. There were other things calling me, and although I was a little nervous about the move to Pisa, and sad to be leaving Sam, Hannah and Peter, it was time to take the next step.

Sam drove me to the airport, and as I was about to go through the customs barrier, she said: 'I'm much happier knowing that I'll see you again soon.'

'Me too,' I said, and we gave each other a final hug.

CHAPTER 3

Getting to know Pisa

The school had arranged for me to share a flat with an English girl called Lisa. I knew nothing about her except she had been in Greece the previous year and was arriving on the ninth from La Spezia, a naval town some sixty kilometres northwest of Pisa. We were to meet each other at the flat at 8 pm.

I took a taxi from airport, feeling tired and a bit low. When I arrived at the flat, I found it locked, empty and in darkness. I waited, and after a few minutes an Italian woman arrived with the keys and lengths of extension cord. She chatted away, clearly unfazed by the fact that I couldn't follow what she was saying. She plugged the cord into a small lamp, ran it through the hallway and out of the front door and disappeared. Seconds later the lamp came on. By now I had understood some of what she was saying: *niente elettricita'* – no electricity!

Lisa, together with her *fidanzato* (boyfriend) Gianni,

arrived at nine. Lisa, in fact, arrived a couple of seconds before Gianni, lurching headfirst through the open front door: 'Damn! Oh bloody hell . . .'

'Hello,' I said. 'You must be Lisa.'

I couldn't see her very well in the dim light, but I noted she was shorter than me and had long blonde hair. Gianni was wearing some sort of naval uniform. I extended my hand and Lisa, by now composing herself, shook it in response. Gianni smiled and said, '*Ciao.*'

'Sorry,' said Lisa. 'I didn't see the step. Why are you sitting in the dark?'

'I've no idea,' I replied. 'The landlady tried to explain something to me, but I didn't understand what it was.'

They went to investigate and established from the landlady, who'd introduced herself as Cristina, that the school hadn't confirmed our arrival, so she in turn hadn't contacted ENEL, the electricity company. We would be in the dark, with no hot water, for two days.

Lisa and Gianni were going out to dinner. 'It's our last evening,' she explained. 'Gianni's ship leaves at dawn. I'll see you tomorrow morning.'

There were two bedrooms which seemed to be similar so I chose one, pulled a few things out of my suitcase, had a quick wash in cold water in the bathroom, which was in between the bedrooms, and went to bed. As I lay watching the garden lights from the house next door flickering on the ceiling, I wondered – with that shiver I always experienced when facing the unknown – what the following day would hold. I'd only seen Lisa for a few minutes, but she seemed friendly and I felt we would get along fine. I thought about my life, and the way I was doing things out of sequence: having babies young, and now flat-sharing. Life doesn't come with a book of rules, I thought as I drifted off to sleep.

At seven o'clock the following morning, I was shaken into consciousness by rattling glass and vibrating air, as though a hand grenade had exploded outside my window. Bloody hell. Was there *never* any morning peace in Pisa? What was it this time?

I shot out of bed and raced to the front door to see the back of a navy Fiat 500 Bambino disappearing up the drive. I could make out the silhouette of the driver, a short person with a cascade of medium-length curly hair. It was the land-lady, Cristina. Later, when I tactfully mentioned to Cristina that the car made rather a lot of noise, she said proudly: 'Yes, it's the 1950 model, reputed to be the loudest of them all.' The idea that the noise might be disturbing me didn't occur to her.

I returned to my bedroom and saw, in the morning light, that it was large, with white walls, high ceilings, two double wardrobes, a desk and shelves. All the furniture was made of varnished, walnut-coloured wood. The floor was chips of granite, of many different shades of burgundy and pink, sanded back, sealed and polished to a finish that shone like a skating rink. The two-metre high double windows looked out onto the driveway and the neighbour's garden. It was a lovely room: light and spacious, and once I'd invested in some floor rugs, cushions, prints for the walls and earplugs, it would be cosy – and quiet – as well.

I went to investigate the rest of the flat. The living room, which doubled as the dining room, had two very ugly easy chairs with heavy floral print upholstery and curved dark wooden frames. There was a plain square dining table with chairs and a matching sideboard crammed with white perspex crockery. The walls were hung with tapestries that looked like ersatz nineteenth-century family portraits. I had no doubt they had been lovingly worked by someone in Cristina's family. The TV on the corner cabinet only received one channel – in black and white – and crackled alarmingly.

The kitchen was off the sitting-dining room. It was small, more like a galley than a real kitchen, with a gas stove, stone sink and fridge. Above the sink was a large white cupboard. I opened it to find it was one huge plate rack full of plates and saucepans. What a good idea, I thought. You wash up, stick the things straight in the cupboard and leave them to drain out of sight.

At the other end of the kitchen, behind a floral curtain, was an enormous pantry with rows and rows of shelves. Through the pantry window I could hear a faint quacking sound. What was it? I went out to see. Round the other side of the house, under the shade of a bay tree, I found a pen of five or six excited geese.

There were two houses on the property, one that fronted onto the road and the other at the end of the stone drive-way. We had one of the three ground floor apartments in the house away from the road. The floor above, which ran the length of the house, was the family home of the landlady. In the course of the next nine months, I learned Cristina's habits well as I lay in bed listening to her clip-clop to the bathroom in the small hours, or take a shower before she went to bed.

Lisa and I had our own small patch of garden, but most of the large garden with trees and lawn belonged to the house on the front of the block, where Cristina's mother-in-law lived. This was my first introduction to a fundamental Italian concept: that families live close together.

Although our flat wasn't high on style or luxury, it was comfortable and characteristic, in a good area and only ten minutes from the centre by bus. The rent was reasonable and Cristina friendly. When we compared notes with our colleagues later, we realised that we'd done very well indeed.

I retraced my steps to the flat and found Lisa getting breakfast in the kitchen. In daylight I could see that she was slim and pretty, in her mid-twenties, with quick, precise movements – a coiled spring of latent energy. 'Help yourself to food,' she said. 'We brought some stuff with us yesterday. There's a general store a couple of doors down, so shopping won't be a problem.'

As I made myself a cup of tea, I asked Lisa how she'd found herself in Pisa.

'By accident,' she replied.

'That makes two of us.' I said. 'Tell me more.'

She'd met Gianni, she told me, while she was teaching at La Spezia. He was a navigator in the Italian navy and had been a student in one of her classes. He'd recently been posted to the Middle East, so Lisa had looked for a teaching job in a place with an airport so they could visit each other in the Christmas and Easter holidays. They planned to set up home together at the end of the academic year, in July. 'Pisa was the first school that offered me a job,' Lisa told me, 'so I took it. And what about you?'

I gave her a brief run-down of the last few months, and explained that I wanted to have a quieter life and be nearer my daughter and granddaughter.

'Good grief,' she said. 'Are you a grandmother?'

'Yes I am.'

'But you don't look old enough! I've never shared with a granny before.'

Lisa, who'd been in touch with the school over the last week, explained that we had an introductory workshop at the sister school at Livorno starting at 10 am. Livorno, a port town some twenty kilometres west of Pisa, is noted for its ugly post-war architecture and chaotic traffic. 'We'd better go,' Lisa said. 'It'll probably take ages to get there.'

I was confused. There was nothing in my information package about a sister school or a workshop, but Lisa seemed to know what was going on so, although she was half my age, I let her lead the way.

We took a bus to the station. Italian buses are punctual and efficient, but the purchasing of tickets is not. We went to the *tabaccaio* (tobacconist, which also serves as a café or bar), and waited in line with the other customers for nearly fifteen minutes. When our turn came, the assistant shook his head and said something quickly to Lisa.

'Damn!' she said. 'They haven't got the tickets we need.'

'What shall we do?'

'We'll have to get the more expensive ones.'

Once on the bus, Lisa showed me how passengers were supposed to insert the ticket into the onboard machine that validated the ticket with a stamp. In a town like Pisa, where just about everyone knows everyone else, fare evasion is unthinkable. Lisa and I, however, were known to hardly anyone, so when we discovered that our salary of millions was barely sufficient to live on, and certainly didn't run to unnecessary bus fares, we travelled for nine months on one unstamped ticket each.

Fifteen minutes later we arrived at the station to catch the train to Livorno. Nowhere is it more evident that clarity and streamlining are Anglo concepts than at an Italian railway station. Booking offices cater for everyone, whether it be a simple query or complex travel arrangements. We found ourselves behind a man whose journey negotiated the length and breadth of Europe. The booking clerk looked up the connections manually, keyed the information into the computer and, after an interminable wait, printed tickets for each leg of the journey. These were examined in detail, first by the clerk and then by the passenger.

It's useless to plead with other passengers because everyone is in the same situation. The only valid excuse to queue jump is to claim a desperately sick parent or child. Although tempted, I was never brazen enough to do it, except on the one occasion when it was true.

Having bought our tickets, we stamped them in the little yellow machine in the station concourse. Ticket inspectors on trains claiming *le multe* (fines) from unsuspecting foreigners with unfranked tickets are one of the more familiar and less reported sights in Italy.

We missed our train and arrived late. So, we discovered, had everyone else.

Tom Mowbray called the room to order and then said: 'I'd like to observe a moment's silence for . . .' He nominated an unknown Italian male. With that, he pushed the play button on the tape-recorder in front of him, and a badly recorded version of the slow movement of Mozart's clarinet concerto swelled forth. He closed his eyes.

I was bewildered. What was going on? Was there to be no explanation? Evidently not.

Tom spoke again: 'Now we're going to play a little game where we all get to know one another. Let's form pairs, and take it in turns to describe an idyllic situation – the setting, the people, what you are doing . . . create something lovely. Two minutes each and then swap.'

I was paired with him. He spoke of his wife, her beauty, her talent . . . of a marine setting with sunshine and gently lapping waves, of his glass of chilled wine . . . no, perhaps a crisp *chianti*, of her tomato juice *condito* with lemon, no . . . Worcester, with ice . . . He closed his eyes again.

I began to feel nervous. It was reminding me of a scene from an eighties comedy in which a little old lady, stuck on a plane next to a young man who insisted on telling her – in minute detail – the story of his slushy romance, finally hanged herself rather than listen to any more. I started to giggle at the memory, but was saved by the Director of Studies, Jim, a tall fellow with a beard, who called time. I hadn't said a word.

The rest of the morning was devoted to presentations by other teachers (interesting), and what I can only describe as more getting-to-know-you exercises. It was a good opportunity to meet the other teachers in an informal setting, but I couldn't help feeling that an hour in the pub would have done the trick just as well if not better. They were a mixed group – mainly English, but also American, South African, Australian and one New Zealander – ranging in age from early twenties to late fifties. Women outnumbered men by something like three to one. I was relieved that they seemed so open and friendly.

On the train back to Pisa, Lisa gave me some background on language schools in Italy. They had boomed in the seventies and eighties she told me. Professional people, who had almost all learned French at school, were now required to speak English to their colleagues in the European Community. Entrepreneurs saw the opportunity, and language schools appeared in the centres of almost every Italian town. Anyone who could speak English and stand up was a prospective teacher. The schools were of variable standard, but not the pay – it was uniformly low.

Lisa also knew a fair bit about the English School in Pisa from an old university friend who had taught there two years before. All the eighty or so English Schools in Italy were part of a franchise, she explained. Tom owned Pisa and Pontedera (a small town twenty-five kilometres east of Pisa in the direction of Florence); he also had a share in the school in Livorno. His first wife had died and he'd only just remarried. His new wife was, apparently, much younger than him, very beautiful and quite mad.

Lisa had already been in Italy for a year and spoke excellent Italian. She'd also taught in Greece and Korea (horrible – rats used to come up the plughole in the shower). She had far more local and professional knowledge than me and I often had to ask her for help and advice. We had different work hours and formed different friendships, and often Lisa went to stay with Gianni in La Spezia, but we were similar types – both interested in books, films and politics – so the little time we did spend together at home was companionable and friendly.

My first lesson was at 6 pm that same evening. I took the bus which arrived at the school at 5 pm. I wanted to prepare myself as well as I could. As I walked down the lane and into the dark entrance which led up the stairway and into the school, I suffered a major hit of nerves. This is madness! I'd signed on for a job I hadn't done before in a foreign country where I barely understood a word.

Jim's large figure loomed at the top of the stairs. 'Welcome!' he boomed in a loud, confident voice. 'Come up, come up. I've got everything for you here.'

He took me into the staffroom and showed me my desk and cupboard space, and gave me my timetable and registers. Each lesson, he explained, was two hours long with a ten minute break in the middle: 'If you get stuck,' he said, 'you can usually find me in the secretary's office. Oh, and by the way, no speaking Italian in the classroom, at least' – and here he grinned – 'not when Tom's on the prowl.'

He must be joking, I thought. By then I had about a hundred words of Italian – barely enough to order a pizza, let alone have a conversation.

I looked around nervously. The walls of the staffroom were painted a hideous sick-room green, made more bilious by the fact that there was no natural light. My colleagues, most of whom I recognised from the morning's workshop, were busy working away at their desks. They all seemed highly professional and efficient. I didn't want to confess that I had no foreign-language teaching experience and didn't really know what I was doing, so I started looking through the course book for my first lesson – a group of six students who'd already studied English for a year.

The time for the lesson was rapidly approaching. What if I couldn't make myself understood? Well, I thought, I'll certainly know more English than the students, and it wouldn't be the first time I'd had to bluff my way through a situation. So looking far more confident than I felt, I walked down the corridor to my classroom, opened the door, walked briskly to the front, smiled and said:

'Hello, I'm Susan, and I'm your new teacher.'

I needn't have worried. Italians are open and friendly and a pleasure to teach. The course book used for the lesson was well written and well structured, so I was guiding rather than teaching. To make it even easier, the students were well versed in grammar and literature, a point not lost on me as an ex-state high school teacher.

The students in this group, as in the other classes, were mostly in their twenties and thirties. During the lesson I asked one student, a particularly articulate young woman called Anna, if she'd been to a private school. She looked horrified. I learned subsequently that Italy has an excellent state school system. Private schools, run by the nuns, are only for slow learners or delinquents.

Towards the end of the lesson Massimo indicated that he'd like me to turn off the ceiling fan which was operated by what looked like a toilet chain dangling down. In my haste I tugged too hard, the chain flew out of my hand and I lurched backwards, treading on a small, round electric foot-operated switch behind me. Simultaneously, the lights went out and the tape recorder started playing the Mozart from the morning workshop, only this time at about a million decibels. Order was quickly restored. I hoped the students – all of whom were now openly grinning – didn't think me a complete clown.

When the lesson finally ended, I felt exhilarated. It had been absorbing and I'd enjoyed myself.

The next morning I decided to check out the local shops. There was a small *alimentari* (grocers) on the corner two doors down. It opened early in the morning, just after 7 o'clock, but then closed for most of the afternoon. The grocers, an elderly couple, wore white tunics and moved at the speed of mud. Much of the produce was exotic and unknown to me – cheeses of all types, salamis from unheard-of places, wines, waters and oils – all pricey and served in slow motion. Added to this was the grocers' habit of chatting to each and every customer at length and in detail. I had forgotten that shopping could be considered a social activity.

The other option was to take the bus which went directly to the supermarket, did a turn of the block, and came back again every fifteen minutes. Lisa and I decided to take it in turns to get rolls and milk for breakfast from the local *alimentari* (where we could also hear and practise Italian), and do the major shopping at the supermarket.

In general, groceries, coffees and eating out in Pisa are reasonably cheap. Anything from the chemist, however, is shockingly expensive – $7 for ten aspirin, for example. The only benefit is that all the assistants in the chemists are trained pharmacists, so are really helpful with advice and don't mind occasionally handing out something without a prescription.

My next chore was to get an Italian SIM card for my mobile phone. I asked Lisa to write what I had to say on a sheet of paper, and caught the bus into town. I chose one of the mobile phone shops at random. Inside was a fug of tobacco smoke, and a fug of people all talking at once. It was here that I learned one of the most important lessons about surviving in Italy: do not, under any circumstances, let anyone get in front of you in a queue. Forget anything your mother or teachers told you about being polite, taking your turn and not pushing in. If you don't stand your ground, they'll all have a go, pretending they can't see you and shoving you out of the way with their elbows. Queue jumping in Italy is a national hobby and done in the most shameless fashion. The only remedy is for you to move faster and shove harder than they do. Believe me.

As I hadn't yet learned this valuable lesson, I waited my turn, patiently, and in the queue. When I noticed the second person push in front of me, I took action and pushed back. *'Mi scusi,'* I said, loudly and purposefully.

The person, a squat older man considerably shorter than me, pretended not to hear.

'Mi scusi,' I said, raising my voice even louder, and giving him a little push with my hand.

He couldn't pretend any longer. He turned towards me, and I glared at him, eyeball to eyeball, until he wavered, and then took a step back to let me take my rightful place.

The shop assistant was smoking, talking on the phone and ringing up the till at the same time. He looked completely frazzled. Finally my turn came. I read slowly and carefully the words Lisa had written for me: 'I'd like a SIM card for my mobile phone.'

'Si', signora, quale tipo?'

Okay, I'd got that. What type? I shrugged. How many types were there?

He looked at me, exasperated, and said: 'Okay, *facciamo cosi'.* And with that he got an A4 sheet of paper out of the drawer under the till, pushed it at me, and went on to serve my enemy, who was treading on my heels at this point.

I looked at what the shopkeeper had given me. It was like a hire purchase agreement – hundreds of questions and even more fine print. It would take a day to work out what it all meant. I folded it neatly in four, put it in my handbag and left.

I showed it to Lisa when I got home.

'That's complete rubbish,' she said. 'You just need to buy a prepaid card and then you don't have to bother with all that paperwork. *'Una scheda telefonica prepagata'* – she wrote on a slip of paper.

Not for the first time I felt grateful that I shared with someone who knew how things worked.

Email access, my final task for the day, proved easier than I'd hoped. There were three computers at the school available for teachers, and if they were busy, there were a number of Internet cafés nearby.

The staffroom was the hub of the school, and certainly the most entertaining club in town. I think the light-hearted banter and general good humour and cooperation came from the fact that we were all away from home and all depended on one another. The twenty or so people on staff fell into three groups: the young ones, recently graduated, looking for fun and overseas experience; the more-or-less middle-aged like me, washed up from other occupations, and the north Americans. The latter mostly worked part-time at the artist colony in Pietrasanta (thirty-five kilometres west of Pisa), carving beautiful Carrara marble into strange shapes to sell to their compatriots back in America. They were casual teachers at the school, doing mainly conversation classes, and were generally regarded as eccentric by the other teachers.

Angela, a large Canadian in her thirties with a maniacal laugh and tight, tight black leggings, was a case in point. She'd been allocated the *bambini* class (four- and five-year-olds),

almost certainly because Jim couldn't convince any of the
contract teachers to take it. Italian children are precious, and
their parents even more so. Everyone tried to avoid them. One
concession, however, was that the children's teacher
got priority on the one-and-only VCR, which was there as a
back-up – if you ran out of ideas, you could show a video.
Angela didn't seem to have any ideas at all. Her constant
shouting at the children in Italian could be heard from the
staffroom: 'Watch the TV! Come on now! Watch the TV!'

One day she was moving the children from one classroom
to another. 'Line up against the wall,' she screamed in Italian.
'Come on, line up.'

'Oh God,' said Lisa, 'she's going to shoot them.'

Angela left soon after, following complaints from the
parents. Shouting and bad humour towards children are
regarded very seriously in Italy. So is wearing black leggings if
you're very large.

Tom Mowbray was a busy man. He had three schools to
run as well as belonging to a number of professional organ-
isations. Most of the day-to-day running of the school in Pisa
was left to Jim and the secretaries. When Tom turned up, it
was usually for a reason.

One afternoon when I arrived to do my daily preparation,
he was standing in the doorway of the staffroom: 'I believe
there have been some difficulties with the photocopier,'
he said.

'Yes,' said Poofta Bastard, sotto voce, 'it doesn't fucking
work.'

Poofta Bastard, as he was called by the younger staff, was

tall with arched eyebrows, one higher than the other, and a new hairstyle every week. In his early forties, he'd been in management back in Melbourne, and had run into financial problems. The exact nature of his difficulties was never made explicit, but the fact that he'd worked in the casino was generally taken as a clue. He'd escaped to Pisa to study Italian with the Dante Alighieri society who rented a classroom from the school. He found himself the only student, and without a teacher. So the school offered him a casual position taking English conversation classes, and from there – in the space of a week or two – he had graduated to the status of a fully qualified teacher. Within a month he was driving round in Tom's son's car.

Occasionally official-looking letters would arrive for him at the school. They all received the same treatment – a resounding rip as they were torn in two before being cricket bowled into the bin. His penchant for Carabinieri – a branch of the Italian police with flashy black and red uniforms – saved him from deportation, and also got him an Italian work contract. This allowed him to stay in Italy permanently, and gave him pension entitlements. But one day he went too far. His old dad back in Melbourne was, he claimed, in intensive care following a heart attack. He had to go to him immediately. His students and colleagues, distressed and saddened, sent emails of hope and encouragement. The more fervent arranged for masses to be said.

As it transpired, he had been offered a lucrative two-month contract teaching in Sardinia for the naval academy, an offer too good to refuse. Even the Carabinieri couldn't save him this time. He got the sack, but shortly after found a part-time post at the naval academy, and was last seen sailing out of Livorno harbour on the *Amerigo Vespucci*, the three-mast naval training ship with three hundred sailors and – reportedly – a grin on his face.

A photocopier is the most crucial piece of equipment in a language school. Nearly every chapter in the teachers' instruction book begins with the words: photocopy one copy of this page for each of your students. No photocopier, no lesson. You can do without a classroom, blackboard, video, tape-recorder, even table and chairs, but not without a photocopier. At the English School, the photocopier broke down continually and continuously. Teachers came to blows over it, accusing each other of having corrupted it in some way. Teachers sneaked in at night to do their photocopying, and when it was working, the word went round faster than a bushfire.

'Well,' said Tom, 'we'll have to see what we can do.'

A few days later it was announced that teachers could take their material to the *copisteria* (commercial photocopier) favoured by the school. There was, however, a snag. Shops in Italy open early in the morning, close for three hours for lunch (1–4 pm), and are usually closed on either Monday mornings or Wednesday afternoons. It was proving a nightmare for teachers to find a convenient time to do their photocopying. I was nominated to go to Tom and express our communal difficulty. And so I learned, for the first time, how things really work in Italy.

Tom looked pensive when I explained our position to him. 'What about a new photocopier?' I suggested.

'We have a three-year contract on our present photocopier,' he replied. 'There's nothing we can do until the end of that period.'

'But it doesn't work.'

'We still have to pay.'

'Even if it doesn't work? Why don't they come and fix it? Surely you aren't obliged to keep paying for something that isn't yours and isn't working?'

The explanation defied logic. The contract had been negotiated by his wife's brother, who worked for a photocopier company. The company had gone out of business and been taken over by another, which was refusing to acknowledge its obligations to previous clients. Any pressure from Tom would reflect badly on his brother-in-law. It was a lesson I was to learn time and again in Italy. In a country where people rarely move from their place of birth, relationships – particularly between family members – are considered more important than logic, financial expediency or anything else. There was nothing to be done: we were stuck without a photocopier.

CHAPTER 4

Settling down

After six weeks I was beginning to settle in to the new rhythm of my daily life: breakfast with Lisa, then a bus trip into town to shop for fruit and vegetables at the outdoor market or look round the weekly Wednesday morning market that blocked three streets with its stands of colourful junk. I was home to cook a lunch of pasta with meat or fish and salad by 1.30 pm, and then I'd read, take a little walk round the neighbourhood and start preparing for the evening lessons. Although the first stretch of teaching was tiring because I was having to adjust to giving instructions and explaining grammatical points simply, I was beginning to look forward to my evenings spent in the company of small groups of friendly people. This lifestyle, with lots of time to myself and virtually no pressure, was allowing me to do things I wanted to do: look around, think, read, discover things and have time to write it down.

The weekends, however, were different. Many of the

younger teachers continued with the habits they'd acquired as students, and spent their weekends in the pub or disco. I was still being cautious around alcohol, but in any case my raging days were well and truly over. So I joined the older contingent – John, Isabella, Rachel and Bill, plus whoever else might be around – in more sedate activities. On a typical Sunday we would meet at the coach station at noon, take a coach either to the seaside or one of the outlying villages about half an hour away and stroll around in the weak autumn sunshine, working up an appetite for what was to follow: a traditional Italian Sunday lunch. It would begin with *antipasto misto* – small, delicate titbits like salami, the local wild-boar pâté, olives and vegetables preserved in oil, or mussels, clams and tiny sea snails cooked in white wine and garlic that you scrape out with a toothpick, or tiny grilled sardines.

Primo piatto, or first course, was pasta – with tomatoes and basil, meat or wild-boar sauce – or a thick local soup made from *farro*, a grain similar to barley that has been cultivated since Roman times, or a vegetable soup with beans. *Secondo piatto*, main course, was usually beef, lamb or rabbit, or fish such as mullet, tuna or weaver, a nasty little critter of a fish which buries itself in the sandy shallows of the Mediterranean, leaving exposed only a line of sharp spikes for unwary bathers to tread on. The poison evidently hurts like hell for a few hours but doesn't do any lasting damage. Although Isabella explained that they always clean the weaver fish very carefully before cooking it, and that the flesh is soft and delicate and quite delicious, I could never be convinced to try it.

Dolci, or sweets, were usually light: ice cream, cassata or fruit salad. Finally came coffee, *grappa* and brandy. By then it would be close to five o'clock, time to stagger to the coach stop for the return to Pisa and a quiet evening in front of the TV, which now displayed a clear, bright (although unfortunately still black and white) image and the choice of over thirty channels, thanks to being connected to the outside aerial.

My first experience of Italian television was a shock. While I expected Italian TV to express different cultural tastes and values, nothing had prepared me for what I saw. During an innocent quiz show a well-groomed, grey-suited, fifty-year-old host with a Hitler moustache sat at a glass-topped table putting questions to contestants. Under the table, and clearly visible through the glass, languished a real live Barbie doll. She was wearing a short, tight black dress from the top of which fell handfuls of surgically enhanced bosom. Her head, with its lustrous blonde tresses, was held just at the height of the host's knees. It must, I thought, be horribly uncomfortable for her. She tossed her head – a dangerous manoeuvre under the circumstances – and her bright red plumped-up lips opened and closed like a fish. I was mesmerised. Was she preparing herself for some lewd act, or was she merely breathing through her mouth to avoid the stench of the host's socks?

'What on earth's going on?' I demanded of Lisa.

'That's nothing,' she replied, 'you'll be seeing far worse!'

She was right. Semi-clad females are used in Italy to advertise and 'enhance' anything and everything, from political programs and football matches to quiz shows and the endless rounds of glitzy variety shows. Apparently it helps the ratings, and no one seems to mind. Well, the men certainly don't mind, and the women, when you ask them as tactfully as you can, shrug their shoulders. They seem to think it's just part of modern life. Apparently, many families encourage their daughters to participate for the money. I never found an Italian willing to comment on the ethics of it, or to consider whether or not it was a good role model for young girls.

Winter was approaching. Although the days were still sunny and warm, the evenings and nights were getting distinctly chilly. My sole possessions were the twenty kilograms of luggage I'd brought with me from Australia. As I'd intended to stay a maximum of three months, and knew I could borrow warm things from Sam in Ireland, the clothes I had with me were light summer things. I had to get some warmer gear. As my budget was tight, I asked around and discovered that there was a Saturday morning flea market just outside the walls of the city.

When I got there I walked up and down the rows of stalls looking for likely items. Eventually I found some grey wool pants in my size and indicated that I wanted to try them on. The stallholder, who was dark and had the flashing eyes of a gypsy, gestured to the back of a transit van. Gracious, I thought, it's the first time a young man has invited me into the back of his van.

Have you any idea how difficult it is to put on and remove

trousers when you can't stand up straight or sit down? It was ludicrous. Only a midget could have done it comfortably. I struggled, pulled and heaved. Finally, after much swearing, I managed to get the things on and done up. I didn't need a mirror to tell me they were no good. The legs ended somewhere between my calves and ankles. I'm tall for an Anglo woman, but a giant by Italian standards. Everything I looked at was too short in the arms or legs, and anything that wasn't too short went round me twice. In the end, I opted for two pairs of Levi cord jeans which would do for work as well as home, a couple of men's poloneck jumpers and a smart navy wool jacket off the secondhand rack. It wasn't quite the kit I used to wear to the office in Sydney, but for the moment it would have to do.

Jane wrote to me regularly. I loved to get her letters full of Sydney news and gossip. Sometimes she'd enclose amusing clippings from the paper, which I pinned on the communal board in the staffroom. Our flat didn't have a phone, so I kept in touch with my kids and sisters by email and text messages, and with my father (who refused to have anything to do with computers) by public phone and mail. The communication with Paul dwindled, but we still sent occasional messages. I made a shrine of family photos above the desk in my bedroom – a habit I'd acquired at boarding school – which I gazed at while I was working. Photos are important to me. I need to 'see' the people I'm close to; I've even been known to have conversations with them. But despite being a long way from my family and friends, I was happy in Pisa.

Where I am is important to me. I love to visit London, for

example, the place of my birth. There's always something to do and each area has a texture that is different and exciting in its own way. But I couldn't live there. It *squeezes* you: the crowds, the cost, the dirt, the anonymity and the grey, penetrating cold. My initial response to Pisa hadn't changed. Its historical ambience and the physical beauty of the place had captured me. It was love at first sight: an affair of the heart, not the head.

I was determined to improve my Italian, this lilting language with its rolled r's and melodic cadences. I bought books and tapes which I listened to whenever I could. Teaching English, I discovered, wasn't the best way to learn Italian. Apart from being mentally tired, a heavy concentration on English grammar seemed to render my brain incapable of absorbing Italian. For example, one morning a young woman approached me in the street: 'Laura?' she asked.

'No, no – *sono* Susan [I'm Susan]'.

She shrugged and walked off.

Later it came to me. *L'ora*, pronounced Laura, means 'the hour'. She was asking the time! How could I have been so stupid?

Stories of such mistakes were commonplace, and the staffroom was where they circulated: there was Simon, who had asked for *cipolle* (onions) instead of *spiccioli* (small change); Bill, who'd confused *coniglio* (rabbit) with *conchiglia* (shell), and a best-ever gaffe, famously reported from the British Institute in Florence, where one teacher asked a shop assistant for directions to Palazzo Stronzi (arseholes) instead of Palazzo Strozzi.

I asked around to find an Italian who wanted to do exchange conversation. One of my colleagues, Jennifer, knew of someone who had recently graduated and hadn't yet found a job. She – Sandra – had spare time and wanted some English lessons. Perfect. Sandra had studied English for six years at school. However, like many school learners, she'd had little opportunity to speak the language. I had very little Italian, so conversation would be difficult. Instead, we agreed to do a 'tandem': one hour of conversation in English for her, followed by a one-hour Italian lesson for me using a beginner's course book.

We met in Sandra's flat, a large ramshackle place on the fifth floor of the bank building next door to the school. The two-person lift, as ramshackle as the apartment, only went to the third floor. I decided to walk the full five flights, and was rendered so out of breath that Sandra, who was tall and slender with chestnut sleek, shoulder-length hair, introduced herself while I recovered. She came, she told me, from Nuoro, a city deep in the mountains of Sardinia. She had, like many other Sardinians (Sardi) come to Pisa to study, and had met her *fidanzato*, who also came from Sardinia, in Pisa. They had been together for two years.

As we got to know each other and Sandra became more fluent she told me more about her family, background and life. Sardinians are proud and hardworking, but jobs in Sardinia are limited. Most end up studying and then working in the industralialised north of Italy. Sandra had recently completed a masters degree in economics at Sant'Anna, the prestigious postgraduate college of Pisa University. She wanted to find something local because her boyfriend, Mauro, was still finishing his studies in information technology.

We drank thimble-size glasses of *filu' e ferru'*, the lethal Sardinian *grappa* (it means 'barbed wire' in the Sardinian language), and ate *carasau*, flat Sardinian bread with pecorino, the sharp and slightly sweet cheese made from sheep's milk.

One day when I arrived, she was busy packing. She and Mauro were going home for the weekend. She very carefully placed his possessions in one case, and her possessions in another. Why not put some of her things in his case to even up the weight I suggested. Because, came the reply, she was going to stay with her parents, and he with his. It was unthinkable for a couple to stay under the same roof if not married she explained.

'But Mauro's mother comes to stay with you here!'

'Yes, but that's here. Back home no one knows that we live together.'

I marvelled at this situation when I was next in the staffroom. 'Imagine, they must be nearly thirty and can't even stay under the same roof, let alone in the same room.'

'That's nothing,' replied Diane, a New Zealander engaged to an Italian doctor in his thirties doing postgraduate work in Pisa. 'When we go to Abruzzo to stay with Alessandro's mother [a widowed general practitioner], not only do I have to stay with the aunt down the road, but his mother unpacks and packs his suitcase for him!'

Sometimes Italy can appear fifty years behind the times.

Eventually Mauro graduated, Sandra found a job and they moved to Milan. I was sad. She was my first true Italian friend.

Learning Italian has been a slow and frustrating process for me, interspersed with moments of great joy when I realised I actually understood something. At first, watching television wasn't much help. Apart from the irritation of the Misses Fewclothes in almost every program, everything was so fast: people moved their mouths, but instead of recognisable words, out came one long rolling rrrrrr . . . But slowly, slowly, with the help of the images, and by writing down words and looking up their meanings, my vocabulary increased.

I started to buy the local paper, and by choosing the international section where I already knew the context, I found I could make sense of what was going on in the rest of the world. Although I'd learned French (and a little Latin) at school, it didn't help me with Italian because I'd been taught in a very academic way. I can still translate French into English, but I can't ask for directions or order a meal. Lisa, who had a good ear and talent for languages, picked things up much faster than me, and although I didn't want to admit it at the time, it's an advantage to have a younger brain.

Lisa played the violin, practising every day. It was a discipline rather than a pastime, she explained, but something she had come to love. The important thing is to master the use of the bow. It is the weight of the bow moving backwards and forwards across the strings in a deadly straight line that creates the beautiful tone. To do this, she told me, you need a firm arm and a relaxed wrist – something that looks easy, but takes at least two years of daily practice to master. She didn't want to lose this rigorously acquired skill. Justine, a former teacher, told her of a quintet looking for a second violin. She arranged to play on Sunday evenings, and so it was one Sunday in late November that Giancarlo the first violinist, called to collect her. He was a tall, smiling man in his fifties, with liquid brown eyes and slow but perfect English.

The following Sunday, he said to me: 'If you have nothing to do, come and listen.'

They played at the house of the pianist, Lucia, a slight woman also in her fifties dressed in the classic English style of pleated wool skirt and cashmere twinset, together with a row of tiny cream pearls. I hadn't seen anyone wearing clothes like that since my childhood. She was married to Roberto, a tall, thin engineer who, unusually for an Italian, didn't seem interested in talking to anyone. The house was a grand *palazzo* near the Tower. It was furnished in the same prewar style as its inhabitants – antiques, fake antiques, mirrors and chandeliers – and smelled faintly of mothballs. It resembled a museum more than a family home.

I learned that the house actually belonged to Roberto's mother, with whom they lived. She was a minor aristocrat from Naples – elderly, difficult, and very rich. They lived courtesy of her patronage, another pattern I came to recognise among well-established Italian families. Roberto, being the youngest child and only male, had been – and continued to be – ruled by his mother. Much has been written of the position of the Italian mamma and, although their influence is certainly changing, Italian mothers continue to control their families and households in a way that non-Mediterraneans find extraordinary. One consequence of this is that Italians are more respectful of their parents, particularly their mothers, and see it as their responsibility to look after their elderly parents, usually having them at home and living as part of the family.

The quintet Lisa joined – Giancarlo, Lucia, Hugo the viola player and Enzo the cellist – played works by Schubert and Dvorak. I, as the only observer, settled on a pale blue raw silk covered chair – doubtless of great value but hard on the backside – and listened to the music. They played for an hour or so, finishing with Bach's double violin concerto, which swirled up to the seven-metre high ceiling of the *salotto* (drawing room) and into my heart.

Term finished two days before Christmas. The staff mostly left for their countries of origin and I went to Ireland to stay with Sam. Hannah – now toddling around and getting into everything – seemed pleased to see me. We celebrated a traditional Christmas, with too much eating and drinking and the occasional bracing walk in the sharp, dark Irish winter. On New Year's Eve we drank champagne and watched – with more than a hint of nostalgia – the warm and joyous millennium celebrations from Sydney, followed by the grey, disappointing offerings from London.

After ten days I returned to Pisa, a little low. Did I really want to face a term's teaching in the cold winter of a foreign country? Everyone in the staffroom was in the same mood. 'But that's normal,' they told me. 'Just wait till spring arrives.'

In January, Giancarlo invited Lisa and me to supper at a friend's house. How nice! It would be good to have a break from routine and mix in local society. It was also fun to have a dinner invitation from a charming man – even if it was just as the hanger-on.

Giancarlo collected us promptly at 7.30. He guided me to the front passenger seat and Lisa sat behind me, shivering slightly. It was a clear night and freezing cold, but as we made our way out into the flat Pisan countryside, the car warmed up and we started to chat. Giancarlo asked me how I'd found myself in Pisa. I told him the story.

He paused. 'But why Italy?'

The answer seemed obvious: 'Well, because it's very beautiful here, but also so I can be closer to my daughter in Ireland.'

'Only an Australian would consider Ireland close to Italy,' he said with a smile.

The supper – for some fifty people – was held in the *cantina*, the old wine cellar. A roaring fire presaged pizza, pasta and *castagnaccio*, a sweet made from chestnuts, pine nuts and sultanas. Lisa and I sat together. Neither of us felt confident enough to start a conversation in Italian, and the Italians were busy chatting amongst themselves.

At one point I caught sight of Giancarlo further down the table, glass of red wine in hand, talking to the women next to him. I liked his open face with its strong, dark eyes and Roman nose – classic Italian features. His steel-coloured hair was thick and wavy, brushed back from his forehead. I had guessed him to be about ten years older than me, but I was often wildly wrong at estimating people's ages. At this point, he saw me looking at him and smiled. I felt a glint of recognition. We liked each other.

Fifteen or so adolescents sat at a separate table, chatting and laughing. I was impressed. Anglo-Saxon adolescents, in my experience don't much like hanging around with adults, particularly their parents. But Italian children are considered part of the social fabric right from the start. Babies and small children are taken to restaurants. They fall asleep at the table or in the arms of a relative. At home, they often sleep in their parents' bed and do all manner of things we would consider inappropriate. They are treated with more respect, but are expected to comply with social norms. They can appear spoiled and indulged, but the result is a more integrated society.

Giancarlo drove us back to Pisa.

'*Buona notte*,' he said. 'I hope you enjoyed the evening. I'll see you next Sunday.' He took a little step forward. Was he going to kiss us on both cheeks, the informal Italian greeting and farewell? He stopped, smiled and was gone.

In February the weather turned bitter. The flat, so cool and airy in October, now seemed horribly cold and draughty. The floor covering – granite-marble chip – did nothing to improve the situation. The central-heating radiators were placed under the large (ill-fitting) windows, ensuring that most of the heat went into the garden. Lisa and I sat with the central heating going full-blast, wearing jumpers, scarves and leggings, hugging hot-water bottles and huddled as close as possible to the radiators.

One afternoon Cristina arrived to collect the rent. She stared at us both, rugged up like bears with only our eyes showing.

'Don't sit in front of the window!' she said. Her tone was serious and stern. 'The draught can be very, very dangerous.'

The window, which was fully closed, looked innocent enough.

'But why?'

She looked concerned by our ignorance and stupidity. 'Because you die,' she said simply.

This was my first experience of the Italian hypersensitivity – bordering on hysteria – on the subject of health. Cristina was not the only person to tell me earnestly that to sit in a draught was to court certain death. A generation ago, evidently, the risk was considered so great that no Italian would sit in front of any door or window in winter if it were not completely covered by a thick, lined curtain. I've also witnessed parents wrapping their children up like parcels before letting them out on a mild winter's day. In summer, children are made to wait three whole hours before having a post-lunch dip in the sea, and I've even heard of Italian mammas who carry a thermometer in their handbags just to check if their little ones are running a temperature.

Somehow Lisa and I survived the cold spell, even though we'd concluded that the shock of the subsequent gas bill with its eighty per cent tax loading was more lethal than sitting rugged up in front of the window.

Giancarlo telephoned Lisa. Would she and I like to accompany him to the theatre that evening? he enquired. There was a particular young Italian violinist playing Tchaikovsky's violin concerto. He was sure we would enjoy it. We checked our timetables. We were both free. Yes, yes, we said eagerly. He would collect us at 8 pm.

Five minutes later my phone rang. It was the school. Would I please ring my daughter in Ireland. I thought nothing of it. Sam often rang the school when she couldn't get through on my mobile. Usually one of the secretaries left a message on my desk or rang to tell me she'd called.

'Mum,' Sam said. I could hear distress in her voice. 'Françoise has been trying to ring you. Granddad died this morning.'

I literally dropped the phone. It fell out of my hand and hit the floor with a clang. The battery skidded in one direction and the phone in another. I was trying to put it back together, but my hands were shaking and I couldn't get the two pieces to match.

At that moment, Cristina stuck her head round the door. 'What are you doing?' she asked me.

I showed her the two pieces of telephone and started to cry. 'My father's died,' I sobbed.

'Oh,' she said. 'Oh dear, I'm so sorry. Come along with me. Come on now!'

I followed her up the staircase at the side of the house and into her apartment.

'Sit there,' she told me in a firm yet kind voice. She poured me a small glass full of something sweet and alcoholic, and brought me the telephone. 'Make as many calls as you like,' she said, and then tactfully disappeared into another room.

I rang Sam back. Through my tears we established that there was to be no funeral in Sydney. My father was an atheist, and had donated his body to a local hospital. As there seemed no point rushing back to Sydney, my son-in-law Peter – decent as ever – arranged an air ticket for me to spend a few days with them in Ireland.

I rang the school and spoke to Jim. He was sympathetic. 'Take as much time as you need,' he said.

I then rang Lisa on her mobile. 'My dad's died,' I said. 'I'm going to Ireland this afternoon. I'll be away for a week.'

'Oh,' she said. 'I'm sorry. How awful. Is there anything I can do?'

I asked her to ring Giancarlo and make my apologies. Soon afterwards, she rang back to say that he'd offered to give me a lift to the airport.

I declined. I wasn't capable of normal conversation, but I was touched that he'd made the offer.

The queue at the airport went from the check-in desk to the exit. A group of English school children returning after a skiing trip were making their presence felt. Their good-humoured boisterousness was too much for me.

I walked the length of the queue, pushed in front of the waiting passengers and played my ace card. 'My father's died,' I said in Italian. 'I'm booked on this flight but I can't possibly wait in this queue.' I turned and indicated the adolescents, by now sufficiently bored to have begun a game of 'shove the trolley in your neighbour's shins'.

He nodded. 'Certainly, madam,' he said sympathetically. 'And I'm so sorry about your father.'

As I sat in the plane, first from Pisa to London and then the connecting flight to Belfast, the reality started to sink in. I would never see my dad again. Our jokey farewell in Sydney had been our final farewell. I felt as if a root of my being had been pulled out of the ground, shaken and left hanging in the air.

My days in Ireland were healing, with long phone calls to Françoise in Sydney and Matthew in Christchurch, and reminiscing and crying with Sam. My daughter had seen little of her grandfather as a child, but when she finished school in Cambridge, and before she started nursing in London, she'd spent a year back in Australia. She stayed with Grandad and Françoise for some of that time, and adored them both. My father, for his part, couldn't believe his luck in having a beautiful eighteen-year-old around. He liked having her on his arm, probably because it made him feel young again.

On one occasion, when Françoise was working, he took Sam to a smart restaurant near the water in Watsons Bay. They were the centre of attention – she tall and leggy like a model, he a distinguished-looking older man. At one point, while my father was in the bathroom, a woman leaned across and spoke to Sam. 'Do tell me,' she said quietly, 'who is your companion? He looks rather familiar.'

My daughter, too innocent to understand the subtle nature of the question, proclaimed proudly: 'He's my grandad.'

When my father returned from the bathroom, she told him what had happened. He was miffed. 'Why did you tell her?' he asked. 'You've blown my cover. You should have kept them all guessing!'

I was glad to be with them, and particularly with my granddaughter, who reminded me of the natural cycle of life and death. And being with a toddler didn't allow me too much time for sad thoughts.

I returned to Italy the following week. In my absence my colleagues had been taking my classes, so I expected my return to be seamless.

The first lesson with a group of four students was to prove typical. They presented me with hugs, kisses and a pot plant. Every single one of my students expressed their sympathy in one way or another. One girl even started crying. Lisa had to help me carry the flowers and plants home on the bus. How different this was from the English stoicism I'd grown up with. For me, it was not only touching, but some part of me heaved a sigh of relief. I didn't have to hide what I felt, because Italians *expect* you to be emotional.

The short, sharp Italian winter was coming to a close. I decided to buy a bicycle. Once again, Jennifer proved helpful: 'There's a bike shop in Via San Francesco,' she told me. 'The proprietor's a bit strange but he often has good-quality secondhand bikes.'

The next day I found myself in a cavern-like shop with new bicycles of all shapes and sizes hanging from ceiling hooks. The walls were decorated with enlarged photos of the Tour de France, and at the back of the shop was a dilapidated showcase crammed full of sporting trophies. After a moment, a man appeared from a recess next to the showcase. He was wearing full cycling regalia: tight-fitting sports shirt, black lycra cycling pants and cycling shoes. I judged him to be in his sixties – perhaps more – greyhound thin with leather skin that spoke of decades spent outdoors. My eyes were drawn to his bulging cycling pants. Had he emptied a bowl of fruit into the front of them?

'What can I do for you?' He spoke with an accent that I now recognised as pure Pisa.

He had only one secondhand bike to offer me. It was sturdy, a luminous and disgusting green colour, with no gears and only one working brake. In a place as flat as Pisa, the missing brake didn't matter too much I decided. I paid 80,000 lire ($80), and named it *il cavallo verde* – the green horse.

Cycling on the right-hand side of the road didn't present a problem. Many of Pisa's thoroughfares are one-way, but this is largely ignored by cyclists, who travel at will and without censure. I concluded that the traffic police, a seeming remnant of the fascist era with their frequent roadblocks, fines and total lack of pity for transgressors, simply couldn't be bothered with the thousands of cyclists who daily flouted the road rules.

One glorious spring afternoon full of gentle heat and promise, I decided to go on a bicycle jaunt round town. I cycled down one side of the river, past the marble fairytale church on the south bank, over the bridge near the old city wall and all the way back up the other side. I wanted to see how far I could cycle along the river bank. After ten minutes, the road gave way to an open park with a dirt track running through it. It looked safe so I kept going. A little further on, the track opened out again and there on the left was a very old church. I gave a little yelp of surprise. The lean on the square, red-brick tower was even more marked than its famous sister tower. I had discovered the second leaning tower of Pisa.

The noticeboard next to the locked doors told me that the church and adjoining monastery had been built between 1152 and 1171. The original monks went round barefoot, hence the name of the church, San Michele degli Scalzi – St Michael of Those Without Shoes.

Everything seemed to lighten up with arrival of spring. Even work – which had dragged somewhat in the cold, dark evenings – was more fun. Except, that is, for one particular evening towards the end of term. A group of my students were out on the balcony during their lesson break. A crowd of people had gathered round the parapet of the Ponte di Mezzo below us and in the background we could hear the ambulance sirens coming along Lungarno from the hospital. Everyone wanted to see what was going on.

One student, Anna, a dark-eyed beauty in her early thirties, let out a small shriek, fled back through the classroom, down the flight of stairs to the front door, out into the narrow lane and on to the Ponte di Mezzo. Anna was a psychiatrist, and the following lesson we learned that one of her patients had thrown himself into the Arno. She'd caught a glimpse of him as he fell. Previously, she explained, people threw themselves off the Leaning Tower. Since its closure in 1991 for structural work, the river had taken over this macabre role. I didn't think it was quite the moment to mention that I'd found a back-up leaning tower only ten minutes away from the original one.

My colleagues were right. Spring in Tuscany is perfect. One weekend Lisa and I cycled to nearby San Giuliano Terme, a thermal spa at the foot of the local mountains where both Byron and Shelley took the waters. A plaque on one of the buildings proclaimed that Shelley had written the poem *Adonis* there.

Another weekend we rode to Marina di Pisa to eat gelato and sit on the rocks observing the Italians taking their after-noon *passeggiata* along the seafront. One afternoon we sat and watched the fishermen at the mouth of the Arno where the river meets the sea. From elevated wooden shacks they lower huge nets into the water, and then wait. After ten minutes or so, they winch them up. If they're lucky, they catch shoals of passing fishing. We watched for a full half-hour, and saw only one poor eel tossing and squirming in the bottom of the net.

Lisa's boyfriend Gianni sometimes joined us, and it was from him that I first encountered Italy's twin obsessions: soccer and food. He could talk endlessly about both (in Italian or English), and it was difficult to conclude which was more important to him.

I told him that Australians played rugby in preference to soccer. His face fell, but he recovered as he described the local *cucina* (cuisine): the different *carciofi* (artichokes), the local purple ones, best eaten raw, and the larger greener ones, which should be cooked. Italian food, he explained, still remains regional, although many things – pizza from Naples, mortadella from Bologna, for example – are now considered national. Tagliatelle was said to have been inspired by the long blonde tresses of Lucretia Borgia.

Gianni was beginning to sound like a guidebook.

In Italy, no meal is considered complete without bread, he continued. Tuscan bread doesn't contain salt because the food is strong and full of flavour. He gave me some examples, all classic Pisan dishes: eels in tomato and pea sauce, stewed wild boar with olives, snails poached in vinegar with onion and garlic, and fried pig's liver with caraway seeds.

Was he describing Shrek's breakfast?

Butter is used in the north of Italy, and olive oil from Tuscany to the south, I learned. Never, Gianni warned, use regular olive oil. It's full of impurities and 'crep'. Pure, cold pressed virgin oil is the only safe choice.

Italians eat pasta every day. It comes in different shapes and sizes, and there is a rigorously adhered to code that dictates which kind of pasta goes with which sauce. At this point Gianni paused and took a deep breath. He was obviously gearing himself up to say something very important.

'Never, *never* sprinkle parmesan on a sauce made with fish or seafood,' he said sternly. 'Never!'

'But why not?' I asked, all Anglo innocence.

He grimaced. I got the feeling that he'd already been over this ground with Lisa: 'It is,' he said firmly, 'a matter of good taste.'

Gianni was leaving the next day, but in the morning he went out early and came home with a bag of shopping.

'I'm making lunch today,' he told me.

'What are you going to cook? I asked.

'*Ventricino*,' he replied.

I was none the wiser.

'Do you want any help?' I asked.

He shook his head, so I left him to get on with it.

He busied himself in the small kitchen, and within an hour an appetising smell of baking was pervading the house. At one o'clock sharp he carried a groaning platter to the table. The centrepiece was a large sausage scattered with fresh rosemary, surrounded by zucchini, tomatoes and roast potatoes. Gianni cut into the meat with a flourish and a whoosh of steam burst from within. He placed a generous portion on my plate and looked at me expectantly. I took a tentative bite.

'It's delicious,' I told him, and he beamed. 'But what is it?'

'*Ventricino* is a dish my mother loves to cook,' Gianni replied. 'I'll give you the recipe.'

After lunch as he was taking his leave, Gianni pressed a carefully written page into my hand: 'I'll tell my mother you liked my cooking,' he said. 'She'll be delighted.'

When he'd gone, I started to read the recipe: 'pig's stomach turned inside out, 5–6 eggs, grated parmesan and pecorino, minced meat (half pork, half veal), salt, pepper, chili powder'. I had, I realised, eaten the Tuscan equivalent of haggis.

'Lisa! Lisa! Do you know what we ate for lunch?' I rushed into the living room where she was watching TV.

'What?' she said. 'Oh yes,' and she gave me a knowing smile. 'It was good, wasn't it?'

I too shocked to reply. She continued: 'You know, I once tried to cook *ventricino* for Gianni but I left it in the oven too long. When I cut into it, it was like slicing through a hot water bottle. Gianni accused me of trying to kill him. It was the worst row we ever had.'

Would I have eaten pig's stomach – inside out or not – had I known what it was? Probably not. But I had to admit, it was delicious.

CHAPTER 5

Paul's visit

Paul was coming to visit me from Sydney. When he rang
one evening to say that he was thinking of coming for
two weeks over Easter, I was astonished. I'd come to expect
very little action from him, and had assumed that we would
continue to drift apart. I was, however, pleased at the prospect
of seeing him. We'd been close for four years and he was a
link to my life in Sydney. It would also be pleasant to see
more of Italy in his company. Paul planned to arrive the
weekend before Easter. The school term didn't end until
Good Friday, but that still gave us ten days completely free.

I was in the local supermarket buying provisions for our
first weekend together when my phone rang: 'I'm in Amsterdam,' Paul said. 'Alitalia' – literally 'to Italy' – 'is on strike.
I'll ring as soon as I know something.' 'To Italy' wasn't going
to Italy or anywhere else, it seemed, for at least twenty-four
hours.

I waited.

In the evening he rang again. 'Look,' he said, 'they may be able to get me onto a flight to Turin. I'll let you know.'

Turin is four hours north of Pisa by train. I waited.

The morning phone call established that his luggage was lost. By the time they found his luggage, the trains were on strike. It took Paul one day to get to Europe, and a further two days to reach Pisa.

I'd forgotten how tall Paul was, much taller than the average Italian, with that slow smile which made his top lip curl under ever so slightly. It was warm and comforting when he put his arms round me. I really had missed him.

There were still four days of term left, so Paul would be spending the first few days on his own. I'd borrowed a bike for him from a colleague, and the first morning we cycled round Pisa while I pointed out the main landmarks – the Leaning Tower, the medieval square with the old, ornate university building next to the church of Santo Stefano, and the river. We called into the school and I introduced him to my colleagues, and then we went to have lunch at my favourite bar, Café Salza.

The Salza family originally came to Pisa from Switzerland one hundred and fifty years ago. Since then they've been running the best combined bar, café and cake shop in Pisa. They specialise in both savoury and sweet delicacies: little glazed tarts with smoked salmon or caviar, or cherries seeped in liquor set in crème anglaise. Trays of bite-sized delight lie in wait under the chilled glass cabinets, looking like provisions for a teddy bear's banquet. And then there are the ice creams: the creamy flavours of *crema* (made with raw egg), or *tiramisu* (which literally means 'pick me up') or *zuppa inglese* ('English soup', or trifle). The prices are steep at Salza, but it's worth it for the pleasure of sitting at one of the outside tables watching the world parade in front of you while eating truly inspired food. The sense of 'must be doing something' which is so endemic in Anglo culture is almost entirely missing from the Italian scene. It's also not considered bad manners to look at people. The elegantly dressed women and stylish men expect to be looked at.

We settled at our table, having ordered *schiacciate* (a type of focaccia) filled with smoked salmon and egg, and glasses of *chianti classico*.

'So,' I said, 'have you thought about what you'd like to do for the rest of the week?'

'I thought I might go and have a look round Livorno,' he said.

He'd been doing some reading. Livorno, he told me, was interesting from a historical point of view, but wasn't really on the tourist trail, so nobody knew about it. I remembered the English School introductory workshop there. I certainly didn't think it was interesting. I thought it was chaotic and noisy, but then I wasn't looking at it from his point of view.

After lunch we cycled down to the station and Paul took the train to Livorno in search of history. The focus for his research was the English cemetery, the first Protestant burial ground in Italy.

That evening he told me that it had taken him a while to find the cemetery because of the general confusion, and the fact that no one seemed to know where it was. When he finally located it – after more than an hour of trudging round in the heat – he found the gates firmly locked. An elderly lady, with gestures and smiles, indicated that he should enquire at the nearby bar. The *barista*, again with lots of hand-waving, helped him understand that the cemetery was open only on a limited basis. Realising that Paul was never going to understand what he was saying, the *barista* wrote the opening times on a paper napkin and gave it to him.

I looked at the napkin. The times were all inconvenient; they clashed with other excursions we'd already planned and booked. 'I know,' I said, 'I'll ask Tom Mowbray. He's lived in Livorno for years so he probably knows who runs the cemetery. We can take it from there.'

The next day, I consulted Tom: perhaps he had some idea how Paul could gain entry?

'Well, if he promises to give it back, he can have my key.'

Tom had a keen interest in local history, and had been largely responsible for restoring and reviving interest in the cemetery. He'd put a lot of his own money into the project, and had been rewarded with a key.

Paul found what he was looking for, the grave of Tobias Smollett, who had written *Travels through France and Italy*. The inscription on the gravestone, however, was a disappointment. The date of death was wrong. To us, and certainly to Italians generally, such a point is not worth mentioning. Dead is dead, after all. To anyone interested in history, it's nothing short of an outrage. Later Paul and Tom met for lunch and spent a couple of happy hours together discussing how they could amend the travesty of the tombstone.

Meanwhile, I had other things – like work – to be getting on with. Because I'd had commercial experience, Jim had given me what he called 'a company course'. I was teaching 'English for Business' to a group of six local businessmen, each one more elegant and cultured than the next. It was the only class where I made an effort to look really smart. This, given my limited wardrobe and budget, wasn't easy, but I made a point of washing my hair, wearing makeup and generally sprucing myself up as much as I could.

It was in this sophisticated context that I discovered another linguistic trap for the unwary.

The piece we were studying, about the commercial success of Marks and Spencer, looked innocuous. Fiona goes off to do some shopping, followed by an analysis of the company's fortunes and then some statistics. Easy, I thought. It started badly.

'Fiona,' reads Fausto, 'buys all her clothes at Marks and Spencer.' He can barely continue. The others are nudging each other and smirking. Francesco is actually laughing, and no one will look me in the eye.

'Go on,' I say.

He continues: 'Fiona also buys her brass and kernickers in the underwear department.'

How did I miss that one? All of them were now grinning openly.

Fausto, being a gentleman, tried to keep things on track. 'What,' he asked, entirely innocently, 'are brass and kernickers?'

'Let's move on to the statistics,' I said, with more enthusiasm than I felt.

In the break, I rushed into the staffroom: 'What the hell does "fiona" mean?'

'Oh no,' said Luca, an Italian–Candian who was always helpful with translating. 'You didn't do the Marks and Spencer piece!'

He proceeded to give me the polite version of the word '*fiona*' which can be roughly translated as a large, juicy woman's private parts. It is used to describe a woman of exceptional buxomness and loose morals, and is usually accompanied by even wilder and more energetic-than-usual hand-waving on the part of the (always) male speaker.

'It's that times ten,' Luca said.

And I had to go and face them for another hour.

When I got home, Paul and I recounted the tales of our afternoon – his highbrow and rewarding, mine farcical. As we sat together at the table in front of the open window that looked out over the garden, laughing and joking and doing bad impressions of Italians, I thought, this is the element that has always been missing: his being there at the end of the day to share a glass of wine and a meal and have a laugh, or simply to share the experiences of the day.

I had three more days of work before the Easter holidays. It had been a long term and I was feeling the need for a break from teaching which, although enjoyable, was intense and tiring. And then my phone rang. It was the secretary from the school. Jennifer was ill. Could I cover her lessons the following afternoon, as well as doing my own four-hour evening shift?

I hesitated. I didn't want to – *really* didn't want to – but it was an unwritten rule that we helped each other out in such moments and, I reminded myself, Jennifer had been very supportive when my father died. 'Of course,' I said.

The following afternoon I cycled into town, locked up *il cavallo verde* outside the school and turned into the entrance. There, at the top of the stairs, a punch-up of some sort was in full progress. In the subdued light I could make out two bodies, one partially on top of the other, and four legs kicking and flailing in the air. The language – half-English, half-Italian – seemed to consist of nothing but blasphemy and expletives. As my eye became accustomed to the gloom of the stairwell, I saw that one was wearing a uniform, and the other – the one underneath – was Simon, one of the teachers.

'What's going on?' I shouted to Simon up the stairs.

'Get out of the way,' he rasped back. 'He's off his head and he's got a gun.'

That was enough for me. I raced outside, and called the secretary on my mobile. She'd already heard the ruckus, and had phoned both Tom and the police.

All I knew about Simon was that he was Welsh, in his thirties, sports mad, and was a respected teacher. Later, he gave us the full story: the previous year he'd been teaching in a small town between Pisa and Florence, and had begun an affair with one of his students. She was the wife of the local policeman. He'd moved to Pisa to escape the situation, but the wife didn't want to let him go. The husband found out, and had come to Pisa to kill him.

Lisa voiced my thoughts: 'Simon,' she asked, 'why did you

go for the only woman in town whose husband had a gun and wouldn't hesitate to shoot you?' What she should have added is: in a country where crimes of passion are frequent and have only recently become illegal.

He looked sheepish and said: 'Sorry everyone. Big mistake that.'

The class – when I finally got there – consisted of *principianti* (beginners) who were learning the terms indicating family relationships. The unit in the course book was based on Hamlet, and the family tree looked like a map of the London Underground. The voice on the cassette recording spoke clearly and slowly: 'King Hamlet married Queen Gertrude and had a *son* called Hamlet. King Hamlet, young Hamlet's *father* died and Queen Gertrude, Hamlet's *mother*, remarried King Hamlet's younger *brother*, Claudius, young Hamlet's *uncle*. Hamlet was Claudius' *nephew*. Hamlet was in love with Ophelia, the *sister* of Laertes and daughter of Polonius. Laertes, her *brother*, was also the *son* of Polonius.'

The students stared at me blankly. This was a new course book which I hadn't used before. It seemed the writer was, frankly, taking the piss at the teachers' expense.

I drew a family tree on the board and we quickly established parents (mothers and fathers), siblings (brothers and sisters), children (sons and daughters) and grandparents (grandmothers and grandfathers).

I pointed to the gap for 'grandsons' and 'granddaughters'. 'Any idea what words go here?' I asked. I thought they might be able to work it out.

Silence.

'Well, what's the word in Italian?' I asked.

Nipoti, came the reply.

'Is that for boys or girls?'

Both.

'And nephews and nieces?'

Nipoti, came the reply again.

'For boys and girls?' I asked.

Yes. Italians make no distinction between grandsons, granddaughters, nephews and nieces because they don't have to. They are all children of the family, which traditionally could mean having up to one hundred *nipoti*. Nowadays, however, Italy has the lowest birthrate in Europe – one child per family is the norm. Families of the next generation will look nothing like those that have existed in Italy for centuries.

The next morning, Paul and I were sitting outside Café Salza, drinking cappuccinos and watching the ebb and flow of the morning shoppers.

'Where do all the African men come from?' he asked suddenly.

I knew what he was referring to. It is impossible to sit in a café, stand at a bar or browse in a shop without being approached by a black man selling tissues, lighters and various other knick-knacks. It usually goes like this: 'Buongiorno.' Big smile. '*Vous compra . . .*' While holding out the goods for inspection.

At this point you say: '*No, grazie.*' And they ignore you, insisting that you buy something, until you either give in or get a little firmer (and ruder) in your response.

The Italians, who are unfailingly polite, deal with them

with a brisk shake of the head. But tourists, who are obvious because they look and dress differently from Italians, are considered fair game. I've tried the shake of the head, the 'No, grazie' and the 'I'll pretend you're not there'. They don't work. The only thing to do is look them in the eye and say: 'No grazie. Non mi interessa [No thanks, I'm not interested],' very, very firmly.

No one seems to know if they are legal or illegal immigrants, although rumours suggest that they are part of illegal rackets run from the south of Italy. Their more sophisticated cousins sell fake handbags (Gucci, Prada and the like), and knock-offs of the latest fashions. They set out their goods on blankets outside railways stations and tourist sites. When the police come along, they gather them up and run for it. When it rains, they are on every street corner selling umbrellas. One day, I got caught in the rain and bought a fake Burberry design for 10,000 lire ($10). By the time I got to school some five minutes later, two spokes were broken and it wouldn't fold up.

I went back. 'This is broken,' I said.

'What do you expect for 10,000 lire?' he asked me.

They clearly don't depend on repeat business.

The following day after work, Paul and I had supper in the local pizzeria, a converted candle factory, where they serve crispy, piping hot pizza by the metre. I'd ordered half a metre of my favourite, bresaola (dried, thinly sliced beef) and olives, while Paul went for the 'four seasons' (standard tomato base with four different types of cheese). We were enjoying a cold beer waiting for the food to arrive when Paul told me that he'd met a different, altogether more sophisticated type of *vous compra* outside one of the local bookshops.

I was surprised. *Vous compras* weren't noted for their literary interests. This, he told me, was a little old lady, her white hair pinned up in a chignon, with a pull-along shopping bag.

'Are you interested in literature?' she asked him in perfect English.

'Well, yes,' he admitted. He was pleased at the prospect of speaking English to someone other than me, and to someone who would, perhaps, know something of the local history.

'I thought so,' she said. 'You look the type.'

By now flattered as well as pleased, he didn't feel the rope tightening.

'I have here a book of poems which will interest you,' she said, reaching into her pull-along shopping bag. 'I wrote them myself.'

He was caught. Nothing but outright incivility would get him out of this one. He paid the 10,000 lire.

'So,' I said, 'where's the book?'

He produced a slim volume from his pocket. I flipped through it, reading a verse here and there. It was, without doubt, the worst poetry I'd ever read.

I found out from one of my students that the little old lady is well known in Pisa. She's a retired school teacher, and goes around selling her poetry with the zeal of a Jehovah's Witness. It's not clear if her motives are financial or literary – possibly both. One trick of hers is to hail a passing motorist, who thinks he is doing a good turn by taking her and her shopping home, only to find himself in possession of a *schifezza* (a worthless thing) and 10,000 lire worse off. She came to the door of the flat one day while I was busy preparing a lesson. It was comical because I (being tall) didn't see her (being very short) and went to shut the door. Her foot shot out with the speed of an Inter-Milan forward.

'Signora,' she said, 'are you interested in literature?'

I knew where this was leading, and so – to my shame – I lied: 'I'm sorry,' I said. 'I'm the cleaning lady. I don't have time for literature,' and gently closed the door.

CHAPTER 6

Travels with Paul

On Good Friday, Paul and I took the coach to Lucca, retracing the steps I'd taken eight months earlier. Only eight months! I felt as if I'd lived another life in that time, one that was separate and removed from my life in Australia. Paul was a link with my former life, and having him in Pisa was comforting. Here was someone who knew my history, and had lived alongside me – however tenuously – in Sydney.

As the coach weaved its way round the same hairpin bends that Jenny had taken at breakneck speed, I looked back down over the plains below. I could just make out the Leaning Tower, and the path of the river snaking its way towards the sea. Despite the breathtaking vistas living in Italy wasn't all joy: some elements were annoying, frustrating and even downright stupid. Someone once said that Italy looked like a very poor country inhabited by very rich people. It's true. There's a high premium on looking gorgeous, and being up-to-date with the latest fashions. Cars are also taken seriously; some of the sexiest and most expensive cars, like Ferraris and Maseratis, are Italian.

This level of personal pride doesn't extend to communal areas, though. The very few parks which exist are often badly maintained and the haunts of undesirables. City centres are dirty because people litter the streets without a second thought; uneven pavements with missing paving stones are treacherous to the unwary. And the queues at banks and post offices often snake into the street in the face of the lazy indifference of the tellers. You get taxed at every turn: when you recharge your mobile phone, when you pay your utilities bills, when you breathe. Corruption – to a greater or lesser extent – is endemic in Italian life. Italians accept all this with more-or-less good grace, which seems to stem from an attitude that there's nothing that can be done about it, so why get upset?

Could I really see myself staying in Italy? Then again, could I see myself going back to mortgage repayments, insane working hours and a going-nowhere relationship with Paul? For the moment, nothing was clear, except that I had ten days holiday in front of me and I was going to enjoy it.

By the time we arrived in Lucca, the heat of the day was up, so we strolled round the walls in the shade of the enormous leafy trees before taking refuge in a church. We chose San Frediano and went inside. It was dark and smelled of incense and damp, like most Italian churches. In a side chapel we found an ornate glass coffin with a brown, wizened body inside, hands folded, dressed in a light lace shawl and apron.

The coffin was surrounded by candles and praying women. We approached cautiously. Perhaps we'd stumbled on some sort of cabal. However, it turned out to be the mummified body of Santa Zita, the patron saint of Lucca (also of lost keys and rape victims), who died in 1278. There is a chapel built in her honour in San Frediano's, and once a year they bring her out so she may be touched by the devout.

The praying women looked up. Their expressions told us that we were not considered sufficiently devout or, worse, perhaps not even of the faith, to partake in the ritual body touching. We left hastily, pleased to escape this morbid ceremony, and to be once again in the open air and sunshine.

After a long, Italian-style lunch in the main piazza, we took the coach back to Pisa. The next day was the start of our grand tour – to Florence, Rome and finally Venice. To say I was excited would be an understatement. I couldn't wait to experience these places that I'd heard and read so much about over the years.

The next morning, Paul and I got to the station early to convert our Eurorail vouchers into tickets for the journey. After the usual wait of fifteen minutes, our turn arrived. The ticket clerk wanted to exert his power – or perhaps he just didn't like tourists – and refused to include me on the ticket: 'Your signature isn't on the form,' he said.

At that moment, I made a serious error. 'That's right,' I said. 'Because I live here and wasn't able to sign the form in Sydney. But my name is on the form, and two tickets have been pre-paid.' Instead of challenging him with the force of logic, which comes across to Italians as Anglo arrogance,

I should have acceded to his power by saying, in a surprised tone, something like 'Oh, isn't it? I can't understand why not. They're so hopeless in Sydney!', while gradually leaning forward and pressing my arms against my chest to get as much cleavage in his face as possible.

'We can't issue a ticket without an original signature on the form,' he said.

'Fine,' I replied. 'I'll sign it now.'

'The signature has to be the same date as the original booking.'

I was digging myself in deeper: 'I've already explained why that wasn't possible. This is ridiculous.'

'There's nothing I can do,' he said.

'Fine,' I snapped, 'then take it to your manager and we'll wait here until you can do something.'

At this point, I had unwittingly played my ace card. The last thing he wanted was his manager getting involved. He sloped off, returning with the tickets only when he was perfectly sure we'd missed our train.

Trains in Italy are – contrary to expectation – clean and punctual. We sat in a compartment half full of Italians, half full of foreign tourists, and watched the countryside change from the flat Pisan plains to the dark green rocky hills with small villages clinging to the tops which surround Florence (Firenze). Forty minutes after leaving Pisa, we arrived in this former capital of Italy, and mainstay of the Italian Renaissance.

The first thing we saw as we left the station wasn't, how-ever, a medieval church or a statue by Michelangelo, it was a large, crowded McDonald's. It probably served as a touch-stone for the thousands of Americans who study art history in Florence, or perhaps it was simply a cheap, easy meal for the hordes of tourists.

We walked on. The zone between the station and the cathedral is the commercial and shopping heart of the city, with the buildings reflecting Florence's past glory. The arch-itecture is imposing, with tall, majestic *palazzi* that are under-stated and gracious rather than ornate. Florence is the shopping capital of Tuscany, with showrooms and shops of all the world-famous labels. Tucked alongside them are the local workshops which sell shoes, handbags and all types of leather goods.

We arrived at the Duomo (cathedral) with its characteristic seaweed green and white horizontal striped marble exterior, and admired the famous dome designed by Brunelleschi. We strolled away from the Duomo towards the river and the Uffizi. The queue outside was, we estimated, three hours long, so we carried on towards the river, and crossed by the Ponte Vecchio, the much-painted bridge with its ancient jewellers' shops. We were on our way to visit Palazzo Pitti, the palace of the Medici family, built in 1450 and now a museum–art gallery. For a while it housed the paintings Hitler stole from Florence during the war.

We walked from room to room, at first delighted, then becoming saturated: 'This is like a Roman feast,' I said. 'It's too rich and it's never going to end.'

Paul smiled. 'If you're feeling sick, perhaps we should go outside.'

The gardens, *il giardino di Boboli*, were a welcome contrast. They rolled away from the house, were simple in design, and combined untamed and formal elements in a natural style. We took photos of one of the garden statues, a plump smiling dwarf sitting astride a turtle.

I read somewhere that everyone loves Florence. I, however, do not. For me, it is crowded, overpriced and full of tourists, no matter what the time of year. In summer it's too hot, and in winter it's too cold. We stayed in Florence for only one day. It would take two weeks to do it justice, but there were other treasures on offer and we were booked on the evening train to Rome.

On the way back to the station, we stopped to buy some apricots and ate them on the train. As the rusty, olive countryside of Tuscany sped past, I caught myself looking at Paul and thinking, he's a lovely friend, and I'm lucky to have him in my life, but I can't go back to how it was before. At that point, I fell asleep and slept all the way to Rome.

La bella figura means 'a beautiful display'. It is in Rome more than anywhere in Italy that you feel the force of this concept, not only in the undisputed style and elegance of the Italian men and women as they go about their business, but in the restaurants, bars, shops or just strolling along the wide, gracious Roman avenues. It is a city to be seen on foot because, as someone so rightly said, 'a walk through Rome is a walk through time'.

Paul and I decided to spend four days, including Easter, 'strolling through time'. Our hotel was a short walk from Rome's main railway station along wide, open streets humming with activity even though it was late in the evening. As yet another passer-by bumped into me on the crowded pavement, I realised that our decision to bring small, hand-held bags had been a good one. When we arrived, the proprietor took us to a first-floor room facing a rear courtyard rather than the noisy street. It was light and airy, with turn-of-the century furniture, heavy green silk curtains and matching chaise longue. We would certainly be comfortable here.

'There are lots of people out and about this evening,' I said to the proprietor in an attempt at a little polite chit-chat. 'Is Rome always so busy?'

He stared at me, unable to hide his incredulity: '*Signora . . . Il Giubileo . . .*' His voice faltered.

'Oh yes, of course,' I said, feeling stupid.

It was Jubilee Year 2000 – the celebration of two thousand years of Roman Catholicism.

The door firmly closed, Paul and I looked at each other and started to laugh. How could we have been so daft? Rome would be teeming with tourists and pilgrims. And so we made a decision: we wouldn't attempt to visit St Peter's, the Vatican or the other main basilicas which would be the focal points of Easter. I was disappointed. I was longing to see the Vatican museum which is full of Greek and Roman antiquities, as well as rooms with frescoes painted by Raphael and the glorious Sistine Chapel roof by Michelangelo. But we didn't want to spend our time queuing and being crushed, so the next morning we set off for Castle Sant' Angelo, the huge round stone 'gasworks' which was built to hold the tomb of Emperor Adrian. It sits on the banks of the Tiber, and over the centuries has been used as a fortress and jail. I wanted to see the battlements where Tosca plunged to her death (and which would doubtless bring back the memory of my goat-rutting neighbours in Sydney).

Rome has a wonderful atmosphere. It's the easy blend of ancient and modern in a city that vibrates with life – and an apparent absence of stress even though crowded – that makes it so appealing. We walked everywhere, through the parks, boulevards and round endless beautiful churches. When we were hungry, we ate in the little restaurants and bars near Piazza Spagna at the base of the Spanish Steps. We checked out the latest fashions in Via del Tritone, and threw Australian coins into the Trevi fountain.

We slowed down to watch a street artist, bent over his easel in an attempt to catch the likeness of a fidgeting child: '*Sta' ferma, sta' ferma* [Sit still]!', he snapped.

Whoosh, whoosh went the charcoal. And then another whoosh. He had it. There she was on paper. Smiles all round. The grateful parents were happy to part with a large *banconota* (banknote) to have this moment recorded in time.

'Come on,' said Paul, 'it's our turn.'

We sat together, his arm round my shoulders.

'Married?' enquired the artist. Whoosh, whoosh.

'No.'

Whoosh, whoosh, whoosh.

He'd finished, and indicated for us to come and take a look. It was a gentle caricature of us. We laughed in appreciation, and as an afterthought the artist added a heart with an arrow through it.

The next day we visited the Forum. This is the site of the ancient ruins of Rome that I had sketched in my exercise book at primary school, not believing that any such place had ever really existed. Although it was crowded with tourists, I was soon lost in wonder at the sophistication of this open-air testament to Roman imagination and engineering. We inspected the remains of the temple dedicated to Saturn, and the house of the Vestal Virgins, who were among the most respected people in ancient Rome. The only hitch was that if they lost their virginity, they were buried alive. We followed the roads taken by the Romans two thousand years ago; the tracks from the metal wheels of the carts were still clearly etched into the hard rock. I wondered what it would have been like to live here all those years ago. We looked at the temples and baths and the houses of the noblemen of the city. They all had under-floor heating systems. Pity they can't do something similar these days, I thought, remembering the bitter cold that Lisa and I had recently suffered at home in Pisa.

We walked the short distance from the Forum to the Colosseum. Outside, men dressed as gladiators offered to pose with us so we could take 'realistic' photographs. We weren't desperate to line up with a Russell Crowe look-alike, but we did want to see inside. The Colosseum is enormous. Originally it seated more than fifty thousand people. For many years it was converted into housing and then fell into ruin. But the true impact for me came from the fact that for three hundred years it had been the site of ferocious and bloodthirsty fights between gladiators, criminals and Christians, often with people being torn to shreds by wild beasts. All this was designed to show the power of the emperor and entertain the masses.

Although Rome is a city to be seen on foot, by the third day I was wishing we had a motorcycle or one of the many types of 'mini' cars that you see zipping around the streets. In the morning, we visited the Pantheon, the huge domed building with the façade of a Roman temple which dates from AD118–128. We did one turn of the circular interior, our heels clicking on the marble slab floor, while looking at the tombs of the painter Raphael, and Vittorio Emanuele II, the first king of a united Italy. His was the statue I'd seen on my first day in Pisa! I felt absurdly happy to see him again, even if this time he was lying flat on his back with his arms crossed over his chest, instead of riding his horse.

In the afternoon we took tea at Babbingtons at the base of the Spanish Steps. It is an olde worlde tea rooms that has fed and watered generations of Anglos in Rome, including Keats who used to live just across the way. Two cups of special blend tea cost $24. Either we were paying for a slice of history, or there was something very special – and undetectable – in the tea.

On our final evening we ate at a small trattoria near our hotel, where the food was typically Roman. We had broccoli soup, thick and flavoursome, sprinkled with seasoned parmesan, and then *bucatini alla matriciana* – a tube-shaped pasta similar to *maccheroni* with a sauce made from pig's cheek. Paul also managed to squeeze in a globe artichoke lightly fried in batter which he declared the best he'd ever eaten. All this was helped down by a litre of house red which the waiter informed us was a *frascati* from the nearby hills.

All too soon our time in Rome was over and it was time to catch the train to Venice. The Eurostar, which links Rome and Venice, is positively luxurious. It was, however, lost on us: all that walking in Rome had been exhausting, and we slept for the whole journey.

Nothing had prepared me for Venice. It's unreal – a floating museum largely untouched since the 1400s. People get around by foot or boat, and with not a car in sight, it's like being on a film set. In fact, I expected to see camera crews round every corner, and was surprised when I didn't.

There are any number of exhibitions, art galleries, lovely buildings and markets to explore, but Paul and I were both tired from all the walking in Rome. So we decided to rest our legs and explore the canals by *vaporetto* (water bus). We bought tickets that gave us unlimited rides for two days, and set off to soak up the atmosphere.

The architecture of Venice, especially the ornate, arched windows and domed churches, looks Turkish – certainly eastern. As the No. 82 *vaporetto* chugged along the Grand Canal, I closed my eyes and imagined snake charmers and carpet salesmen instead of German and Dutch tourists dutifully following their tour guides.

The canal system is vast and intricate. Water taxis cover the main routes, and the 300 000 or so inhabitants either have their own private motor boats (there are police boats which power around fining people who break the speed limit), or walk along the little lanes and bridges which border and cross the canals at every turn. Gondolas are for tourists. They are expensive ($150 for a half-hour ride) and the price goes up at sunset, presumably based on the idea that a romantic Venice sunset is worth a week's wages.

Paul and I were hungry. Lunch – panini filled with the local *salame all'aglio* (salami with garlic) – seemed hours ago and we wanted to find a good restaurant for dinner. We chose an area away from the main tourist traps, and looked around for a local to ask. My time in Pisa had taught me that Italians, who are all obsessed with food, are usually only too happy to give a recommendation. Men, I've found, are better informed than women (perhaps because women tend to eat at home), and someone portly (with an obvious interest in food), is going to know more than a stick-insect. We found a chubby, friendly local who directed us to a restaurant just round the corner where, he claimed, you could eat well at a reasonable cost. We had seafood risotto (which the proprietor told us was the typical dish of Venice), together with a pinot grigio from Friuli, the nearby wine growing area. After slices of pear tart and short black coffees, we walked the short distance back to the 'bus' stop and our hotel.

The next day, we again took *vaporetto* No. 82, but this time in the direction of San Giorgio Maggiore, an island opposite St Mark's Square. There is nothing to see on the island except the church of the same name, but the view back towards St Mark's Square is one of the most famous and loveliest to be seen. We were sitting on a bench admiring the view, when an elderly, well-dressed gentleman sat down beside us. His elongated head together with a pointed chin and nose reminded me of Mr Punch.

'Where do you come from?' he asked us. We told him. 'Ah. Australia. If I were younger, that's where I'd be headed now.'

'But why? You live in the most enchanting city in the world.'

'Yes, superficially,' he replied, and then went on to describe a scenario that was as sad as it was bleak. Venice was a victim of Italy's post-war industrial boom, he told us. Nearby plants and factories had altered the delicately-balanced ecosystem. Instead of occasional flooding at high tides, Venice was now subject to floods of at least a metre twenty-or-so times each year. The factories had now been shut down, but the damage was done – Venice was slowly sinking into the sea. Many ground floor shops, offices and apartments were uninhabitable, and without the prospect of work, young people were moving out.

'Within ten years,' he concluded, 'Venice will be a city of old people and tourists. Everyone else will have gone.'

Our energy restored, Paul and I decided to devote our third day in Venice to modern art. *Vaporetto* No. 1 dropped us off at

Ca' Pescaro (*Ca'* is short for *casa*, house, and is used extensively in the Venetian dialect), which, apart from being a
superb example of baroque architecture, also serves as the
Modern Art Gallery. We looked at the glossy, flowing statues
of Rodin (how *did* he get the cold, white marble to 'move'?)
and the kaleidescopic paintings of Gustav Klimt. In the afternoon, it was the turn of Peggy Guggenheim. She'd lived in
Venice, entertaining the famous artists of the time, and had
left her remarkable collection to the city after her death. As we
wandered from Pollock to Chagall, passing Dali, Magritte,
Picasso, Miro' and Braque as we strolled, I wondered if Peggy
ever got fed-up being surrounded by such precocious talent.

Paul wanted some souvenirs to take back to Sydney, so our
final day was spent looking round the street markets and
then on to the souvenir shops on Ponte di Realto, the steep-
angled, Gothically ornate bridge. He looked at ornaments
and trinkets made out of brightly-coloured Venetian glass,
and the wonderfully evocative masks that people wear for the
annual Festivale in February. He decided that the masks were
too delicate to transport (which was just as well because later
I read that they're all made in Taiwan), and chose instead
silver jewellery boxes decorated with tiny glass beads.

After four days of meandering, the final evening of our
holiday arrived. We ate our last plate of Venice's seafood
risotto with a bottle of *prosecco*, and afterwards Paul and I sat
in St Mark's Square at one of the outside cafés, listening to the
string orchestra play 1930s tangos, sipping *grappa* and recap-
ping the previous eight days. We agreed that Italy, steeped in
history, its architecture largely preserved since medieval times,

together with wonderful food, wine and enjoyment of life to the full, had to be one of the most magical places on earth.

As the sun set, we strolled back to the jetty to catch the *vaporetto* to our hotel. We were standing on the jetty, which was dark and crammed with people, when suddenly I felt a shove from behind and the weight of my handbag changed. I was carrying it in front of me, across my body. I knew pick-pockets operated in Venice, which is why I was carrying my bag in a way I felt was safe.

I knew immediately what had happened: 'My wallet! It's been stolen!'

'What?' said Paul. 'But who . . . how . . .?'

I'd seen the girl who'd taken it: she was alongside me on the jetty. She must have unzipped my bag and grabbed the wallet at the same time as her accomplice knocked me off balance. She and her group – two other girls and two men, one wearing a white straw hat – stayed on the jetty for a while before skipping off. It would have been too obvious if they'd run away immediately. I was all for challenging them.

'Are you mad?' said Paul. 'Do you want to get knifed as well as robbed?'

He was right, of course, but I was still furious. I had little money in my wallet, but I had three credit cards, my driver's licence, my Medicare card – things of no use to anyone else, but vital to me and a nuisance to replace.

When we arrived back at the hotel, the receptionist was sympathetic but philosophical: 'Unfortunately, it happens all too often. It gives Venice a bad name. We don't like it.' I didn't like it either.

I had to report the theft of my credit cards immediately, he said, to ensure that the thieves couldn't make any purchases with them. He gave me the telephone numbers. Also, as my only means of identification were in the wallet, I had to go to the police and make a statement. I protested. What was the point? I'd never see the wallet again.

'Because, Signora,' he said a little wearily, clearly having met this objection before, 'in Italy it is illegal to go about without some form of identification.' In the country that spawned the Red Brigade, responsible for civil bombings during the 1970s and 1980s, it is compulsory to carry an identity card at all times, or for foreigners a passport or driving licence.

The telephoning should have been easy, but it wasn't. The recorded message told me that the number had changed, and was now another number, which was said very quickly in Italian. I took down what I thought was the number. It took several attempts to get it right, and then an interminable wait as the line was permanently engaged. Finally I was put through to someone very helpful in America. The entire process was then repeated for the other cards.

So our last evening together was reduced to a shambles. I felt tired and more than a little upset. Paul was leaving for Sydney the next day, and that, together with the loss of my wallet, was making me feel vulnerable. I knew it was an exaggeration, but it seemed as if my ties with home were being shaken loose.

Early the next morning we were off to the police station. There was only one policeman on duty, and he wanted to talk about his wife's cousins in Melbourne.

'Will I see my wallet again?' I asked.

He shrugged. 'It does happen, but it's rare.' The thieves, he explained, are almost always gangs of Albanians who come for the rich pickings to be had during the Easter holidays when Venice is full of tourists. They don't usually leave any traces behind.

He made five photocopies of my statement (I have no idea why), and after I'd signed each one and he'd inspected them all, he gave me one copy to keep. This was to serve as my identity card until I could get a replacement driving licence from Sydney.

It was time to leave, Paul for Sydney, me for Pisa and work. We said goodbye at Venice railway station. We'd spent two weeks together. I would miss him. He gave me one final hug and kiss. 'I'll be in touch,' he said.

'Yes,' I said, 'me too.'

We were parting in the most romantic city on earth, and even though I knew that underneath nothing had changed, I sat on the train speeding back towards Pisa with tears misting my eyes.

CHAPTER 7

Life moves on

The new – and best – teaching term began. There was warmth and energy in the air and the finishing line was, so to speak, in sight. I made two decisions: I was going to move on from Paul and I was going to have fun.

I told Lisa of my resolutions. Being younger, she saw things in much simpler terms. She said: 'Good idea. If you don't want to drift forever, put Paul out of your mind and get busy with other things – and other men.'

'Lisa,' I said, 'it's not that easy at my age. Men don't exactly form a queue for me.'

'No,' she said, 'that's because you're not paying attention. While you're playing safe with Paul, you're not really making yourself available for other offers.'

Was she right? I wasn't sure, but she'd certainly given me something to think about.

I cycled in to school. I had a new class and Jim wanted to give me the register before the lesson began. In the staffroom there was a new teacher, as well as the usual suspects. I caught her accent immediately. An Australian.

'Hello,' I said, 'I'm Sue and I come from Sydney.'

'Hi,' she said. 'I'm Sarah from Brisbane.'

'Is this your first day?' I asked.

She gave a big laugh, revealing the whitest teeth I've ever seen. 'I wish! I've been here for years – I don't want to think how many – but usually I work at Pontedera. I'm just helping out with a few classes in Pisa.'

'Have you got time for a coffee?'

We walked under the wide colonnades towards Café Salza, and heads turned. Sarah was in her early thirties and nearly as tall as me, with honey-coloured hair and blue eyes sprinkled with gold specks. She had the sort of figure that women work out at the gym every day for, and a feline elegance. She, however, didn't seem aware of the attention she was getting. What would it be like to be so lovely, I wondered. Perhaps you'd get fed up with the constant male attention, and it probably made growing older more difficult. I wasn't sure I'd like to be looked at all the time – but then again, I'd never know.

As we sat outside Café Salza sipping Campari and soda (Oooh, lovely, I really needed this), Sarah told me something of her life. She'd worked as an auditor for one of the major accounting firms back in Australia, but had found it all too stressful: 'You wouldn't believe what it was like. Once I was sent to do an audit of an Aboriginal council in the Northern Territory, only they'd all gone walkabout and one of the elders had put a sort of curse round the building so I couldn't get in to see the books. I sat in the stinking heat for three days, and when I got back to the office, they blamed me!'

She lived, she told me, just outside Pontedera with her dog and an Italian flatmate. 'I only came for a year,' she said, 'and then I met a man so I decided to stay for him. By the time that fell through, I'd got a job at the school so I decided to stay for that. Every year I say I'm leaving, and every year I'm still here! One day I'll make up my mind.' She laughed. She seemed the sort of person who would be comfortable anywhere. I felt lighter as we walked back to the school. I liked Sarah: she was funny, relaxed and Australian.

The new class was a group of employees from the university, four bright, bubbly women, one of whom had just had a baby. They were following the international Trinity College syllabus, something I hadn't taught before. It was entirely based on spoken work, and the students had to present a topic and then be questioned on it by the examiner. I didn't know which of ten levels, ranging from beginners to fluent, I should enter them for. I studied the instructions from Trinity, and a colleague from Livorno sent me a cassette with some specimen exams. We listened together in class.

In one example, a Japanese girl, clearly proficient in English but with a pronounced Japanese accent, was talking about origami: 'Twiss er paper like ees, turn over . . . an do agen like ees . . . An ven tell little holes en it . . .'

And, lo and behold, a summer palace.

'I suppose,' the examiner said, a slightly desperate edge to his voice, 'that you can make lots of interesting things out of paper.'

'Less,' she said.

We agreed that origami didn't really lend itself to verbal presentation.

I decided that Level 7 was the correct level, and we spent the following six weeks preparing for the exam. They researched on the Internet while I scanned my old copies of *Literary Review* and *The Economist* for interesting material. Maddalena found an article in *Literary Review* that she liked. It was a review of a biography of one of those mad Englishmen who risked life and limb to collect new species of orchids. It had information on the breeding habits, life cycle and everything else you could ever want to know about orchids. 'I like flowers,' she said sweetly.

Eva was interested in Australia. She asked if I had anything on Aboriginal culture. I found some good sites on the web, and referred her to those. At the next lesson she said, 'The sites were really interesting. But there was nothing on the present day. Could you explain the current situation between Aborigines and white Australians?'

It was a question all Italians asked me sooner or later, and one I had come to dread. I tried to explain how incompatibilities between the cultures, historical factors and some serious government blunders had contributed to the present situation. How perhaps a comparison with American Indians and white Americans was a way of understanding it better. By now, they were all listening. I had to admit that I had, in fact, never visited areas where Aborigines lived and so all my knowledge was gleaned from newspapers and television.

'So,' Eva concluded, slowly and thoughtfully, 'what you're

describing is a basic lack of respect for Aboriginal values and culture.'

There was no avoiding it. 'Yes,' I said. And felt immediately ashamed.

The others chose more pedestrian subjects: alternative health, and the Italian economy.

The exam was to be held at Lucca, not Pisa. They were going together in the one car, and called in to see me on the way: '*In bocca al lupo*!' I said. It means 'good luck' – literally, 'in the mouth of the wolf'.

'*Crepi*!' they replied. Death to the wolf!

I have never got to the bottom of this strange saying. The symbolism suggests Little Red Riding Hood, but no one has been able to explain it to me. However, in Italian you never, never wish anyone *buona fortuna* (good luck), because it brings bad luck.

The examiner – according to them an archetypal Englishman, tall, thin and polite – called Maddalena first. She was with him for twenty minutes instead of the scheduled ten. Her colleagues were getting nervous on her behalf, but she came out with a huge smile on her face. The examiner was an orchid buff who practically lived in the Orchid House at Kew Gardens, and knew everything there was to know about these exotic plants. He was enthusiastic about her presentation, gave her ninety-six per cent as a mark, and then wanted to chat about her research.

In fact they all got distinctions. I told Sarah about it over coffee. 'You know,' I said, 'I feel guilty because obviously I could have put them in at a higher level – Level 8 or even 9.'

'Don't worry,' Sarah said. 'It's the sort of thing you only find out by experience. At the end of the day, they're happy and it hasn't done your reputation any harm.'

I had to go. There were lessons to prepare and I wanted to check my email before the other teachers arrived for the evening lessons. There were four messages: one each from my kids, one from my sister in London, and one from Paul. I opened his first: 'Just to let you know that our division is finally moving to Melbourne. We're trying to get out of it, but it seems that this time it really will go ahead. So by the time you get back to Sydney, I may well have gone south.'

The move had been in the pipeline for so long that nobody took it seriously. Well, now it was looking certain, and despite my earlier resolution, the news unsettled me.

After classes that evening, on the way to the *gelateria*, Lisa and I met one of my students, Giulia, with her parents. 'Why don't you come to dinner one evening?' enthused her mother. 'I'd like you to meet our son, Francesco.' We fixed a date and time.

Lisa and I settled down to our favourite ice creams – mine forest fruits and lemon, hers strawberry and *crema*. 'You know,' I said, 'it's very nice to be invited to dinner by Giulia's parents, but they don't speak any English and my Italian is really basic. It might be hard going.'

Lisa, who'd had lots of experience of this situation with Gianni's parents, gave me a piece of advice. 'Just smile and say yes to everything,' she said. 'It keeps them happy and probably won't do you any harm.'

I thought this reasonable, so in time I duly presented

myself at the *ora di cena* (dinnertime) of 8 pm.

Italians, although chaotic in many aspects of their lives, are rigorously uniform about mealtimes. Breakfast is usually nothing more than a couple of sweet biscuits or *cornetto* (croissants) with coffee. Families have breakfast at home, while most single workers eat it at the local bar, usually standing up rather than sitting down. This takes a maximum of five minutes. Lunch, however, is at home with all the family together. Shops and offices close from one to four in the afternoon, and the school day also finishes at 1 pm, so shortly thereafter everyone is *a tavola* (at the table) for a meal which consists of a pasta dish, followed by meat or fish and vegetables, finished off with fruit and a short black coffee. Never cappuccino. Only Anglos (who clearly know nothing about how to eat well) drink cappuccino after a meal. If the mother of the family is working, which is more and more the case in Italy today, everyone goes to the *nonna* (grandmother). Dinner can be soup, or slices of cold meat and olives, followed by eggs or fish or, indeed, another pasta dish. Lunch and dinner are accompanied by wine and water. Although tap water is perfectly good, people prefer to drink bottled water.

The table, in the neat but modestly furnished dining room, was perfectly laid. Each setting had a crisp, white napkin embroidered with delicate flowers, mirroring the border of the tablecloth. I was sure the gold-rimmed plates and glasses had been brought out specially for the occasion. It was a little awkward at first. Giulia was only in her second year of studying English and no one else in the family spoke English at all. Francesco clearly thought it amusing to have a foreigner in the house, although I wasn't sure why.

'*Sei una buona forchetta?*' asked the father.

I hesitated. I knew how tedious it was explaining things to someone who didn't understand your language. On the other hand, I had no idea what he meant by 'Are you a good fork?' I remembered Lisa's advice. 'Yes,' I replied in Italian, smiling.

He looked delighted and proceeded to serve me the biggest plate of pasta I'd ever seen. He was asking me if I had a good appetite. And so I found myself in front of a mountain of *pappardelle al cinghiale* (long, flat pasta with a wild-boar sauce), together with the expectation that I would eat it all.

I struggled with the fork (no spoon or knife, only a fork), twisting and cutting as best I could. The others finished and I still had half a plateful. The mother was looking a little offended (didn't I like her cooking?), and the father disappointed (had I lied?). I struggled on. A five long minutes later, full to bursting point and with an indecorous brown spray-painted halo around my plate, I finished. The mother and father smiled happily.

They wanted me to coach fourteen-year-old Francesco in English. He wasn't doing well at school. After a couple of lessons, it was clear why. He turned up late, didn't do his homework, and wanted to talk about football, and only football, in Italian.

The weather suddenly turned hot. Our small garden was overlooked by both Cristina and her elderly mother-in-law, who lived in the house at the front of the block. It was fine to sit and read, but Lisa and I certainly wouldn't have felt comfortable sunbathing there. So we started to investigate the local beaches. The closest, Marina di Pisa, could be reached by bike, but the shore consisted mostly of heavy rocks used to defeat the spring tides; there was very little sand. Viareggio, with its miles of promenade, pretty fishing port and swathes of sand, was much more attractive, but a half-hour coach ride away.

One particularly hot morning, Lisa and I were standing at the bus stop when a car pulled up. It was Giancarlo, from Lisa's quintet. 'Where are you going?' he asked. 'May I give you a lift?'

We explained that we were going to the beach at Viareggio, and he drove us to the coach station in the centre of town. 'Why don't you come to my beach one day?' he asked. 'There's a hut for getting changed, showers, and an umbrella and deckchairs. No one uses it during the week and the sea is very nice at Calambrone.'

Lisa and I looked at each other: Calambrone? Beach hut and umbrella? Wonderful! We fixed a day and time and as he drove off I said to Lisa, 'You know, I could get to like this – beach huts and being driven around by a charming man.'

'I thought you said there weren't any nice men in the world,' she shot back.

'I *said*' – emphasising the words as I spoke – 'that there weren't any nice men available for *me*.'

'Well I think he's available,' she said.

'Now,' I replied, 'you're being completely ridiculous.'

Giancarlo arrived promptly to take us to Calambrone, a village fifteen kilometres southwest of Pisa. Travelling along he explained that in addition to the beach hut, he had a holiday home five minutes away by car.

Many families have an apartment in Pisa and a house by the sea. The reason is simple. The summers in Italy are long and hot, and like most of southern Europe, offices, factories and many shops close for the month of August. Everyone decamps to the seaside to avoid the insufferable heat and even more insufferable mosquitoes. This gives Italians – always social at the best of times – another complete set of friends and acquaintances with whom to pass the time of day.

We arrived at 'Bagno Edina', or rather we arrived at the entrance, a huge concrete arch painted a lurid yellow with the name in bright turquoise. How was it possible, I wondered, for Italians with their highly developed aesthetic sense to choose such garish colours.

Giancarlo seemed to read my mind. 'The *bagno* isn't so well managed these days,' he said, 'but my grandfather was one of the first patrons when it opened after the war, so we don't move out of habit and loyalty.' He forgot to mention that the position of his beach umbrella – first row, close to the sea – was considered pride of place, and that he'd have to wait a lifetime to get a similar position elsewhere.

I still didn't know what a *bagno* was, but rather than show my ignorance, I waited. It was a tactic I often used in Italy when I found myself in situations where I didn't know what was going on. Rather than panicking, a better approach was to relax and wait and see. Usually things became clear in time.

We passed through the arch to a sandy carparking area, down a path through the pine trees which opened out onto a number of wooden chalets and beach huts on the sand. Beaches in Italy are almost without exception run privately, I discovered from Lisa, the facilities being leased and managed by a *bagno*. Each *bagno* varies, but usually they provide changing huts, umbrellas, deckchairs, showers, a restaurant, bar – possibly a disco – and various sports facilities like table tennis, volleyball and a form of football played in a large 'cage'. People can either pay on a daily basis, or more usually, for the entire summer. The foreshore – the first ten metres of sand from the sea edge – is considered public, but only for strolling along. If you try and put your towel there, someone from the private *bagno* will come and ask you move. Every resort has one free public beach, which is usually a rocky outcrop fenced off with barbed wire somewhere near the sewer outlet. No Italian would be seen dead in such a place.

'Bagno Edina', Giancarlo's *bagno*, had a simple restaurant overlooking the sea and no disco or computer games. I guessed it was for professional people rather than a younger crowd. Lisa and I were happy. We had a deckchair each, shade, a hut to change in, showers, somewhere to have lunch, and the bus to take us home at the end of the day went from outside the main gate. We thanked Giancarlo, genuinely and profusely, and he left.

'He's nice, isn't he?' I said to Lisa. 'Nothing seems too much trouble. How old do you think he is?' I wondered if she would confirm my guess.

'I don't know,' she said. 'Pretty ancient.' I've noticed that people under thirty consider anyone over fifty to be relic material. 'I think he's a grandfather,' she continued, as if to prove the point.

'A bit like me?' I said.

'Yes,' she smiled. 'Exactly like you.' And then added: 'I don't think there's a wife.'

It was mid-May, and I was to have another visitor. The family had been friends from my Cambridge days, but only the husband, Hans, was coming to visit on his way back to Cambridge from a conference in Trieste. 'Find me a hotel,' he had said, 'not too expensive, and quiet.'

I cycled round Pisa from one hotel to the next, asking to see rooms and enquiring about rates. I decided that the Hotel Victoria would be suitable. It was right on the Arno, central, not too noisy, and decorated in the by-now familiar Pisan bourgeois (*borghese*) style, with marble floors, high ceilings and dark, turn-of-the-century furniture.

Hans is a curious mix. He was born in Germany, and looks like a Viking: tall and muscular with flowing hair. But he grew up in New Zealand (where the family fled to escape the Nazis), and this is reflected in his clothes: brightly patterned Maori shirts, Dr Scholl's, and even the occasional agate necklace. Many years ago, he and his wife moved from New Zealand to Cambridge so he could pursue his career as a scientist.

We had only one full day together, and Hans wanted to visit the Cinque Terre (five lands), which are five little fishing villages on the coast of Liguria, an hour or so from Pisa by train. The villages perch under mountainous rocks which face the sea, and are connected by rail but not road. Because they are isolated, the Cinque Terre have remained undeveloped and unspoilt over the centuries. There are footpaths and tracks which go either along the base of the rocks or over the top, offering some of the best walking in Italy. If you're serious, you can walk the full length, from Monterosso to Riomaggiore, which takes a couple of days.

We, however, had to be back for my evening lessons so decided to walk the two or so hours from Vernazza to Monterosso, with its winding medieval streets, narrow alleyways and beach which promised the possibility of a good seaside restaurant.

'Tell me,' said Hans as we set off along the narrow cliff path, 'what do you make of the Mafia?'

I hesitated. Explaining the Mafia to people from outside Italy is on a par with explaining the Aboriginal situation to non-Australians. 'Well, from what I understand it started off as a code of rules for regulating businesses in Sicily, based on a system of honour and protection of rights. Apparently, in the beginning violence was used only as a measure of extreme last resort. Over time, however, it's degenerated into a sort of bullyboy free-for-all involving and corrupting everything in its path. There are Mafia-type interests in Naples and other areas of southern Italy running protection rackets, prostitution, drugs and other lucrative ventures. There are almost daily killings between rival gangs, and there's almost certainly police and political involvement, too.'

'I guess these things can really take hold in poor areas,' Hans replied, 'and from what I can see of the Italian political system, it's impenetrable bordering on corrupt. Half the politicians should be in prison.'

'Probably all Italians should be in prison,' I laughed, 'because the only way to get anything done is to ignore the rules. I break at least three traffic regulations daily, and I'm probably an illegal immigrant as well!'

'Would you consider a future in Italy?' he asked.

'I don't think so,' I said. 'It's not a country that is kind to single women. It's almost impossible to survive economically on one salary, and social life is based round the family. If you don't have a family, you risk becoming isolated. Also there's no work, and at my stage of life I would be limited to what I'm doing now.'

We continued walking until, hot and thirsty, we descended into the main piazza of Monterosso, which fronts onto a narrow beach. We stood watching the children splashing in the clear, shallow water, regretting not having brought our swimming costumes. Monterosso is set in a bay, surrounded by mountains and rocky outcrops. It is the furthest north of 'the five lands', and possibly the prettiest. A maze of steep, narrow lanes, alleyways and steps lead away from the piazza, twisting and turning to negotiate the difficult terrain. The little houses, with uniformly rectangular windows and violently coloured geraniums cascading from their wooden windowboxes, looked as if they'd been piled one on top of the other by a giant celestial crane.

There was a funeral at the local church. The mourners,

mainly women, were dressed in black. They followed the hearse on foot and then filed into the church behind the coffin. The undertakers, in the meantime, leant against the hearse chatting and laughing and – incongruously – eating ice cream. The church bell tolled resolutely.

We walked up the hill behind the town, past small huts and garden allotments. We wanted to see the view. We walked for a full half an hour without meeting anyone.

'It's strange,' remarked Hans, 'how the towns in Italy are so busy and the countryside completely empty.'

'I'm not surprised,' I said. By now I had understood that Italians are social creatures, with a great love of camaraderie and companionship. They delight in congregating– the men in the bars, the young women strolling together with their infants, the older couples taking a *passeggiata*. You rarely find an Italian alone. The idea of plodding off for a walk on your own would be completely alien, and considered sad. There are more mobile phones in Italy than in America. Truly. They call each other frequently, not to impart information, but to maintain contact. A typical conversation goes like this:

Brrr, brrr . . .

'Hello.'

'Where are you?'

'What are you doing?'

'Okay, see you later.'

'Ciao, ciao . . .'

For a second, my mind flashed back to 'Bagno Edina', the sandy beach, rows of green and white sun umbrellas and Lisa and me splashing ourselves in the shallows of the clear, refreshing sea water to cool off.

'Look at that!' we exclaimed together. We'd both spotted her at the same moment: a tanned Italian beach babe, hair piled on high, up to her waist in water, chatting on her mobile phone.

It was June, the final month of the school year. The students were preparing for either end-of-course exams, or the more frightening international Cambridge exams. I was scheduled to supervise one of the in-house written exams. I had nothing to do except sit at the front of the class and make sure there was no cheating. With only eight students, it would be a doddle. I could read my book for two hours – or so I thought.

I explained the format of the exam (which they all knew anyway), the starting and finishing times, and how anyone found copying or cheating would have their paper torn up. I gave them a couple of minutes to get started, and then turned to my book. I glanced up to find they were all – without exception – obviously and shamelessly copying from each other.

I jumped up.

'Clearly you didn't understand. Copying is not permitted – not under any circumstances,' I said firmly.

However, it was I who had not understood. Italian family-based culture doesn't place much value on individual endeavour. It's far more important to help each other out and maintain the cohesion of the group. Taking exams is regarded as a collective activity, so they copy. And the strange thing is, they don't necessarily bring any intelligence to bear on the situation: it's often the brighter ones who copy the mistakes of their weaker classmates.

The exam finished, I collected the papers and returned to the staffroom.

'You wouldn't believe it,' I said. 'They all copied – every single one of them, right in front of my eyes!'

'Oh yes,' Bill said, 'that's normal. You have to stand on top of them if you want to stop it. It's best to ignore it. And anyway, it's easier to mark the papers when the answers are all the same.'

Term ended. I'd spent nine months in Pisa and now I had to decide what to do next. Lisa was joining Gianni in La Spezia straight away, and I was going to Ireland in August, which left July free. I asked Cristina if I could stay in the flat and she readily agreed.

Lisa and I decided to have a small farewell dinner. We would invite a couple of friends each, and Gianni would also be there to help with the cooking. On the morning of the dinner party, I cycled to the supermarket to get some provisions. I didn't intend to buy too much, but had somehow managed to acquire four bagfuls of shopping. I was struggling with them at the checkout, trying to work out if I could take them all on the bike or whether I'd have to leave two and come back, when I felt someone's breath on my neck.

'Ah,' said a voice. 'We meet again.'

It was Giancarlo. He looked at the bags. How are you going to manage all that? Are you on foot?'

'No, on the bike.'

'In that case, I'll take the shopping and you can cycle home.'

When I got home five minutes later, he was leaning on his car, waiting for me. 'Thank you,' I said. 'That was really kind of you. I bought far more than I'd intended – you know how it is.'

He smiled. 'Yes, it's easily done. But taking all that shopping on the bicycle could be dangerous.' His English, as well as his manners, was very correct.

'We're having a small dinner party this evening,' I said impulsively. 'It's very informal but it would be nice if you could join us.'

'Are you sure?' he asked.

'Yes, of course. It would be lovely if you came.'

He smiled. 'Thank you. In that case I look forward to seeing you later.'

Shortly before eight o'clock the dinner guests started to arrive: Sarah, Bill, Isabella, Diane (the New Zealander) and her *fidanzato* Alessandro. At eight on the dot, Giancarlo arrived carrying two bottles of red wine and an enormous fruit flan. He was dressed casually: dark blue trousers, white shirt and navy sweater thrown across his shoulders. His height and build, together with his easygoing generosity, reminded me for a second – perhaps more a nanosecond – of my father.

It was a warm, still evening and we ate – thanks to the

kindness of Cristina – at the outside table under the fruit trees. In the Italian tradition, men sat next to women, with no one next to their partner. I had Gianni on my left, Alessandro on my right and Giancarlo opposite me. Lisa and I, with Gianni's help, had prepared an entrée of pasta with a fresh tomato sauce infused with basil and mountain herbs, followed by grilled mullet with potatoes and salad – simple but delicious.

The conversation – in half-Italian, half-English – ranged from holiday plans to political intrigues, with the ever-present comments on soccer and food. Giancarlo seemed relaxed and chatted away easily with everyone. Every so often, he lent forward to ask me a question or make a comment, his face illuminated by the candles between us. When he smiled, I noticed little lines radiating from his eyes which spoke of warmth and laughter.

'Are you interested in films?' he asked me.

'It's one of my passions.'

The touch paper lit, we talked cinema – comparing films, describing favourite scenes and laughing and joking about various actors. Before long, the entire table had joined in, with – in fine Italian tradition – the voices getting louder and louder and everyone speaking at once.

Finally, Gianni served dessert – Giancarlo's flan – followed by short black coffees and *grappa*, but nobody seemed in a hurry to leave. I glanced at my watch. It was past midnight – where had the time gone? When I looked up, Giancarlo was studying me. His eyes seemed both tender and yet tinged with something I couldn't quite recognise.

By the time the party broke up, it was past one o'clock. Giancarlo was the last to leave. He said goodbye to Lisa and Gianni, and I walked with him to the gate. 'Thank you for a wonderful dinner,' he said. 'Will I be seeing you again?'

'Well, I'm here for July but after that I'm not sure.'

'In that case, may I have your phone number?'

He wrote it on a scrap of paper and put it in his wallet. And then with the gentlest kiss on the lips and squeeze of my hand, he was gone.

Lisa had a grin on her face – well, a smirk.

'Yes?' I said. 'What is it?'

'You were a big hit there. He didn't take his eyes off you all evening.'

I shook my head. 'Rubbish! You were imagining it.'

We washed up together, and as I put the plates in the rack above the sink, I thought about the dinner party and how well it had gone and, yes, Giancarlo had been paying attention to me. I smiled to myself as I remembered how pleasant it had been.

The next day Lisa and I said our farewells. We'd spent nine months as flatmates and now she and Gianni were off to make a life together. We kissed each other and promised to stay in touch.

The flat felt empty and quiet with Lisa gone, so I invited Sarah to stay for a few days. She was also marking time before going to teach at a summer school in England, and as we'd already decided to do some day trips together, it seemed easier if we were both under the same roof.

Sarah, who'd been in Italy for many years, had gone out

with Italian men. There was a question I was dying to ask her.

'Sarah,' I began, 'all the students I've met live at home.'

'That's normal. Most Italians live at home until they get married.'

'And they've all got *fidanzati* [boyfriends and girlfriends].'

'Oh yeah. In the land of hyper-romantics and close families, there's a lot of pressure to attach yourself young. But they often stay boyfriend and girlfriend for years before marrying.'

'That's my question,' I said. 'Where do they have sex?'

Sarah laughed. 'In the car, of course. Why do you think Italians are so attached to their cars?'

She went on to tell me about her first date with an Italian. He'd picked her up from home, taken her for a lovely meal, and then out for a little drive in the country. The country air set off her hay fever, but she didn't have a tissue. She asked her date if, by chance, he had one handy.

'Look in the glove box,' he said.

She couldn't believe her eyes. It was kitted out like a cross between a chemist shop and an adults only store.

Sarah knew everything about *rapporti* (relationships) between men and women. Italian women, she told me, are focused on looking good and being captivating. They place a high value on themselves, and don't give away their favours easily. They make the men beg. Really beg – on their knees. Once they've got their man, they are often jealous and possessive. That's why foreign women are regarded with such delight by Italian men. They give in easily, and there are no unpleasant consequences when the affair ends.

Men, on the other hand, want the most beautiful woman

they can find on their arm, and reserve the right to play around with other women as much as they like. Most Italian men are assiduous at the chase, but often lose enthusiasm once they've conquered. I could hear the echo of my mother's voice from the past, in one of her rare comments on my Greek father: 'It was fine until I married him!'

An Italian after a woman will do anything for her – take her to exotic places, buy her expensive gifts, cook for her . . . anything. That's why so many Anglo girls go for Italian men. But they often end up unhappy, Sarah told me. Once they're married, and particularly if they have children, things change. The men expect to continue in their bachelor habits – staying out late, going to soccer matches and having other women. Italian women, who place great value on having a family and home, and who in any case have seen it all before, make the necessary adjustments – like shrugging their shoulders. Anglo women married to Italians frequently find themselves trapped and miserable. She was warming to the theme: 'And you hardly ever see an Italian girl marrying a foreigner. That's because Italian women place a high value on social standing and staying close to the family. They want to marry a local engineer or doctor, not some foreigner.'

I thought about it. Perhaps this approach to 'the mating game', so very different from our own, had evolved out of a strict Catholic dogma which preached unrealistically high moral behaviour for both men and women. A generation ago, no unmarried Italian woman would have been allowed out with a man on her own. There would have been a chaper-one of some sort – a brother or older relative. Sexual relations before marriage were considered sinful, pregnancy unthinkable. But there was still a gap. Italian men were and are noted wooers and lovers. How did they learn these skills if not – dare I say it? – at the hands of their women?'

'Prostitutes,' Sarah explained. There were – and still are – many *case chiuse* (brothels) where the girls specialise in initiating young men. A generation ago, it would have been normal for a group of young people to go out together, and once the young ladies had been safely escorted home, the young men would round off the evening with a visit to the local bordello. In fact, the concept is so accepted in Italy that it's reflected in the language: a *casino*, an everyday term used to describe a mess or confusion, literally means 'brothel'.

Sarah had a car – a prize possession for an English teacher. We didn't do much driving about because it was hot and we preferred to just relax, but there was one place I was dying to see. 'Sarah,' I said, 'have you ever been to Torre del Lago?'

'No, but I've heard about it.'

'Let's go,' I said.

Torre del Lago is twenty minutes northwest of Pisa by car, and is the place where Puccini composed his operas. The house he built still stands, set in a lush garden overlooking the lake. The maestro himself is buried in the chapel of the house, and his spectacles rest on the piano where he wrote many of his famous operas. I'd seen *La Bohème* in Sydney, and wanted to know more about its composer. Nearby, and still overlooking the lake, is an open-air opera theatre where every July and August they stage a festival of Puccini's music. They were playing *La Bohème*. I just had to see it performed in such a perfect setting.

During the day, Torre del Lago could be any sleepy Italian village but during the evenings of the festival it is transformed into one of the most elegant and sophisticated places in Italy. Women wear long, flowing gowns, their shoulders draped with silk shawls to protect them from the slight evening chill, their thick wavy hair held back with glittering clips. The men wear tailored suits or black smoking jackets, their shoes and hair brushed to a lustrous gleam.

My wish was granted.

Sarah and I booked tickets for *La Bohème* for the last Saturday in July – my last evening in Pisa. We had great fun getting dressed. Sarah wore a long black skirt with a matching sequinned top and delicate pointy-toed shoes. I wore a shimmery coffee-coloured full-length number with a roll neck which I'd pounced on at the secondhand stall in the weekly market. It was a clear, balmy evening, and as Rudolfo and Mimi sang their love for each other, Sarah and I sat under the stars with tears in our eyes for the beauty of the singing and the hope of love to come.

The next day Sarah took me to the airport. We kissed and hugged each other. 'Bye, mate,' she said. 'It's been great. See you very soon.'

CHAPTER 8

Ireland and then . . .

I flew to Belfast from Pisa, this time rejecting the drinks and snacks offered to me by the blue-suited hostess who looked about fifteen years old. Sam collected me from the airport. The air was warm and humid, with a distinctly unpleasant farmyard smell. I guessed it was the muck-spreading season.

'Phew!' I said. 'What a whiff!'

Sam smiled wryly. 'Yes,' she said, 'Isn't there just?' Her tone was flat.

Hmm, I thought. Something's wrong.

We drove on through the bright green countryside. I commented on the sharpness of the colour.

'It's green,' she said, 'because it's *always* wet.'

Hmm, something really was wrong. Experience, however, had taught me never to enquire directly but to bide my time. Sam would tell me when she was ready.

July is the month of the Marches in Northern Ireland. This is when the Protestants celebrate their historic victory over the Catholics in who-knows-which century by marching with bands and flags through the Catholic areas in certain towns.

This year the violence had been worse and gone on longer than usual. I do believe – like the situation in the Middle East – that if you don't come from the area you have little chance of understanding what is really going on. But to my eyes, the Marches looked like an attempt by the Protestants to lord it over the Catholics, and for the Catholics to vent their humiliation and anger. There seemed to be a fair measure of yob violence thrown in as well. Everywhere I saw signs of 'the troubles': graffiti – coarse and alarming – soldiers in the streets, flags in gardens, and even national colours painted on the kerbstones.

'Don't go into these areas,' warned my son-in-law, pointing at the local roadmap.

'But why not?' I asked. 'It's got nothing to do with me.'

'Your English accent,' Peter said. 'It would only take a couple of words . . .'

I was appalled, but came to realise that it was true. There was no sitting on the fence round here – you were on one side or the other, even if you didn't want to be.

Sam eventually confessed that she wasn't happy in Northern Ireland. Although they were doing well financially, she hated the politics. I felt for her. She wanted to bring her daughter up in an easy and relaxed way – rubbing shoulders with everyone. They had, she told me, thought about it carefully and decided that they'd have a better future in Australia.

They certainly would, and it would be wonderful for me to be able to see them without having to get on a plane. But

I knew there were plenty of hoops still to jump through. Sam wasn't born in Australia and neither was Peter. They would have to go through the whole immigration rigmarole, with no guarantee of success. I wasn't going to get my hopes up just yet.

'You could always come back with us,' Sam suggested.

I was considering what she'd said when the phone rang. It was Tom Mowbray, once again completely out of left field: 'We need a teacher for a business course we're running in September and October. Would you be interested?'

'Yes,' I said without hesitation.

The timing was perfect. I still hadn't reached a definite decision about what to do next, whether to return to Australia permanently or spend another year teaching in Pisa. Two more months in Pisa would give me time to make up my mind. As I lay in bed that evening, watching the long Irish twilight finally give way to the black of night, I recalled the farewell dinner in the garden and Giancarlo leaning towards me and smiling. At that moment I realised that going back to Pisa wasn't just a convenient arrangement, it was something I really wanted to do.

The next day I rang Jim, the Director of Studies at the school in Pisa. He took care of accommodation and I had nowhere to live. Jim referred me to a Signora Barani, who lived in Via Roma, the narrow road that leads up to the Leaning Tower and down to the river. 'I don't know what it's like,' he said, 'but a few teachers have stayed there over the years.' I rang Signora Barani and, after a brief introductory chat, I booked a room.

At the end of August we celebrated my birthday, and shortly afterwards Hannah's. I had great fun constructing a cake shaped like a '2' and decorated with Bob the Builder, Smarties and two candles of course. She wasn't at all interested in the cake but loved the candles, puffing and blowing and trying to touch the flames. When I left, she put her forehead against mine and gave me a damp, sticky 'Maori kiss', rubbing her nose backwards and forwards against mine; then she pulled her head back and shrieked with laughter.

I sat on the plane and watched the European landscape pass below: the patchwork greens and browns of France followed by the dramatic Swiss Alps, like row upon row of grey cardboard egg boxes sprinkled with icing sugar. What makes Europe exciting is the sheer variety of languages, customs, cultures and history – the elements I loved and appreciated in Pisa.

The plane banked to the left and flew down over the sea where Lisa and I had so happily swum, before finally turning inland and flying in low over the industrial port of Livorno. As we came into land, I thought of Hannah back in Ireland, and the ache I felt every time I left her. If Sam and Peter succeeding in migrating to Australia, it would certainly give me a compelling reason to return to Sydney.

Pisa in September shimmered with warmth and light after the dismal grey of Northern Ireland. Despite the noise and chaos, it also felt remarkably peaceful. My new landlady, Signora Barani, was short and a little stooped, with dark tinted hair that made her face look unnaturally pale. Speaking slowly as if to a child, and with an accent I couldn't place, she explained that I would be staying in the former *cantina* – the wine cellar. As I followed her to the far side of the large entrance hall, I wondered if Italian was her first language. She unlocked what looked like a broom cupboard and led me down a narrow, low-ceilinged corridor. To the left was the galley kitchen and bathroom. To the right, the bed-sitting room. It was sparsely furnished, spacious but damp, without a single ray of sunlight. The rent, however, was reasonable and – I told myself – I would be out a lot, so it didn't matter about the light.

I called in to the school to collect my registers and information for the course. Main term didn't begin until October, so the only staff around were Jim and a couple of others who were still teaching summer courses. They were all in a cheerful mood. The summer courses involved comparatively few hours of teaching and the stress of full term was still over a month away.

The business course I was teaching was for managers of a local pharmaceutical company, and the lessons were held in their offices near the station. The building was a *Viareggina*, a grand three-storey sand-coloured townhouse with solid stone balconies and deep green shutters, set in a small garden with trimmed hedges and giant palms. I signed in at the security desk, collected my visitor tag and was escorted to the second floor. The lessons were held in the boardroom, a large room with frescoed ceilings and a vast chandelier. I never quite got used to discussing English grammar in this setting. I kept expecting – like Phantom of the Opera – the chandelier to crash onto the heavy round oak table and crush us all to pulp.

The group comprised three marketing managers and their director – all men, immaculately dressed in business suits. The only remarkable thing was that one of them, Luca, who I guessed to be in his early thirties, was completely bald and hairless as an egg.

We worked hard perfecting grammar and trying to eliminate the sing-song intonation which, although charming, gives Italian English a comic touch. The lessons, normally quite structured and formal, relaxed when the rather stitched-up director was on one of his frequent trips to Rome. On one such occasion, Luca began to talk about his life outside the office.

Three years ago, he told us, he'd met a Russian girl. (I was too polite to ask where or how; Russian girls often start off in Italy as prostitutes.) They'd gone out for a while, got on well, he'd been to Russia to meet her family and eventually they'd married.

I looked at Ernesto and Ivano to see if they'd heard it all before, but they both looked as intrigued as me.

One day, he continued, he'd been taken ill at work. 'I felt very sick,' he said, 'and decided to go home.'

'I arrived home and found her in bed . . .' He hesitated. 'With another woman.' He paused while the impact of this statement sank in. 'And then *this* happened.' As he spoke he rubbed his bald head. 'A couple of days later my hair started falling out, and within a week I didn't have a hair left on my body. It was the shock. I've had everything – injections, therapies . . . nothing works.'

No one spoke. And then Ernesto shrugged his shoulders.

People shrug their shoulders a lot in Italy. It means, never mind, tough luck, thank God that wasn't me, there's nothing you can do about that one, mate.

'And your wife?' I asked. (I couldn't restrain my curiosity.)

'I threw her out,' he said. 'If it had been another man' – he paused again – 'but a woman!'

I shrugged.

Sarah returned back from England in the third week of September. I was pleased to see her. Work was keeping me busy, but the staffroom was quiet and I missed having someone to laugh with. We arranged to meet at a small trattoria on the corner of Piazza Dante and Via Arancia where the food was local, the proprietor friendly, and didn't mind that we stayed long after we'd finished eating.

She looked as lovely as ever as she swept into the restaurant, offering *buona seras* and her perfect smile all round. At that moment I realised that Sarah – with that smile, vivaciousness and ready laugh – reminded me of Sam.

'How was the summer course?' I asked her.

'Hell,' she said. 'Complete hell.'

She made a face like she was sucking on a lemon:

'I was teaching in the mornings, doing sports and outings in the afternoons and then had to supervise dormitories at night. I had thirty Italian teenagers – all hormonally-overdosed and trying to get at each other. Thirty! I ask you. How was I supposed to keep an eye on all of them? By the end of the first week, I was so exhausted I fell asleep before nine o'clock. When I came to at midnight I decided to do a quick check of the dorms. They were all sleeping, except Bruno and Elisa who were going at it like rabbits. I rushed in and started prising them apart. You should've heard them! Embarrassment? Remorse? Nothing! They called me all the names under the sun, and then Bruno threatened to report me for not doing my job properly!'

We laughed. I could just imagine Sarah's indignation in the face of such shameless behaviour.

'Have you heard from the charming professor?' she asked with a sly smile.

'No. He has my phone number but nothing. Do you think I should ring him?'

'No!' Sarah said, very firmly. 'This is Italy. It's his call. You just have to wait.'

'Well the course ends in a few weeks and then I'm almost certainly leaving for Australia. If he's interested he'll have to get a move on.'

I enjoyed being with Sarah – she had great optimism and called things as she saw them. She could also drink. We'd eaten pasta, with a bottle of *chianti*, and then her favourite: *vin santo* (a strong, sweet wine) into which you dunk *cantuccini* – almond biscuits – which, she reckoned, could get you nicely tipsy without appearing to drink anything at all.

At the end of September, I went to pay the rent. Signora Barani's flat was on the first floor. I knocked, but she didn't answer. The door was ajar. Perhaps she hadn't heard. I pushed open the door a little wider. She was in the *salotto*, curtains drawn, and on the large wooden table in front of her candles flickered into her face. Her sleeves were rolled up, and as she moved towards me I saw the blue-black numbers etched into her arm.

'Excuse me for disturbing you,' I said, trying to cover my shock. 'I wanted to give you the rent.'

'Will you take a coffee with me?' she asked.

I accepted, although part of me wanted to escape what I knew was to come.

She was Polish originally, she explained. She had met her husband in Auschwitz. He brought her to Italy after the war. She was a widow with one son – a good boy – who worked for the council. 'Have you read Primo Levi?' she asked.

'I've read *If This Be Man*.'

'And what did you think of it?'

For once in my life, I was without words. How could I – a person not even born during those times – pass comment on Levi's haunting first-hand description of daily life in Auschwitz? But what was worse, I knew she was really asking for a comment on her life – what did I think of how it had been for her? Like Levi, her life had become a constant celebration of those terrible, terrible times. And for her, as for him, there was no escape.

'Signora,' I said, 'I can only say that he was a man of great perception and a very fine writer.'

'You have kind eyes,' she said. 'Come and see me again.'

It was now almost November and soon the two months would be up. My reasons for being in Pisa – to be nearer Sam and Hannah, to restore my health, and to have the experience of living and working in a foreign culture – had been met. I had recovered, the family was planning to move to Australia, and I'd had a brilliant year in Pisa. I hadn't heard from Giancarlo, but then again, had I really expected to? In any case, my thoughts were turning towards Sydney. My ex-colleague and 'casual' tenant (who'd been renting my flat for over a year) had found a place of his own and was moving out in a few weeks. But the main thing on my mind was my father. While I was in this place so far from home, I could sort of pretend that he was still alive. But he wasn't, and I needed to face up to reality. I would return to Sydney, get a temporary job and save up to visit Matthew and Rachel in Christchurch.

Sarah and I met for one last supper and chat at our usual restaurant. Our dinner was a little subdued. It's always sad to lose a friend, and there's something about the foreign experience that makes friendships more intense. It's like you haven't got forever to get to know each other, so you cut through lots of layers and just get on with it. But with our usual pasta and red wine followed by masses of Sarah's favourite *cantuccini* and *vin santo*, we were more cheerful by the end of the dinner.

We left the restaurant and were standing in the lane outside. It was time to say goodbye. I gave Sarah a big, theatrical kiss on the cheek. We were both giggling. As I lifted my head to plant the second one on the other side, Italian style,

I saw, over her shoulder and outlined by the light of the restaurant, Giancarlo.

'Ah, *buona sera*,' he said, and smiled.

'*Buona sera*'. A pause . . . 'You remember Sarah?'

'Yes, of course. How are you?'

'Very well, thank you. We were just having a little farewell dinner.'

'Oh really? Who is going where?'

'Me,' I said. 'I'm returning to Sydney next week.'

'In that case,' he said, 'please have dinner with me before you leave.' He got out a little black diary. 'What about Thursday?'

That was my last evening. What better way to bow out? 'Yes,' I said, 'thank you.'

And with more *buona sera*s all round, he walked off.

Thursday evening arrived. It was raining. No, it was pouring: *pioveva a dirotto* – raining cats and dogs. The doorbell rang.

'*Buona sera*,' he said and, gesturing towards the rivulets of water, 'It's a pleasant evening, isn't it? The car's just outside.'

The raindrops ricocheted off the pavement and into my shoes. We drove out of Pisa towards the coast. I could see only water through the misted windows. I hope he can see where he's going, I thought.

We talked amiably about the things we had in common: Lisa and her plans, the *bagno* at Calambrone, my colleagues at the dinner party back in July, and his quintet. He was an easy conversationalist and a ready listener. Any fears I'd had about stilted conversation evaporated as we settled into easy chatter

– mainly in English, but with the odd Italian phrase thrown in. We were going to a restaurant at Torre del Lago, if it was all right with me. He hadn't been there for a while, but had heard recently that it was very good. How strange. This was the same place that Sarah and I had spent such a magical evening together at the opera.

We arrived at the restaurant, a small chalet-like building with a wrap-around verandah overlooking the lake. We sat near the open log fire. The waiter, who moved as if he were on ice skates, brought us the menu.

'Is there a local dish?' I asked.

'Well, the seafood antipasti are good,' he replied, 'and then there's wild boar cooked with chocolate and pine nuts.'

It sounded exotic. 'Fine,' I decided. 'I'll have that.'

The seafood antipasti were served in oval bowls piled high with mussels, clams and other shelled creatures I'd never seen before. It's like picking your way through a graveyard, I thought, as I prised open the next shell to find a tiny, furled sea-animal inside. I tried to spear a clam with my fork. The result was like one of those Chinese martial arts films: it shot across the plate, hit the side of the bowl, flew into the air, did a couple of somersaults, and landed *plonk* right in the middle of the white damask table cloth.

'Oops,' I said. What else was there to say?

Giancarlo laughed and touched my hand. 'Don't worry, you've done the next customers a favour. They'll have to wash the tablecloth now instead of just putting it back in the drawer.'

A few minutes later, the wild boar arrived accompanied

by a bottle of local red wine. It was a dark meat in a rich, gamey sauce that dissolved in my mouth. As we ate, I realised that it was years since I'd had dinner with a man in this context: one where he knew little of me, and I little of him, and yet something had us drawn together.

'What's life like in Australia?' Giancarlo asked.

I tried to paint a picture of the relaxed, open lifestyle that I associate with Sydney, and mentioned my family, and how I'd never imagined having them at separate ends of the world.

He smiled as I spoke and occasionally leant forward and touched my hand. 'Children,' he said, 'never do what you want them to.'

Ah, so he had children. He went on to tell me that his wife had died some years before, and he had two sons who were both married and lived locally. 'And', he said, 'I have one grandchild.'

'Well,' I said, 'at least we're on the same footing there.'

When I asked him if he enjoyed teaching violin, he looked surprised. 'What makes you think I teach music?'

'I heard you telling Gianni you were a teacher and I just assumed it was the violin. You're so involved in the quintet . . .' my voice trailed off.

'No,' he said. 'Music is a love and a hobby, but I'm an economist – I specialise in European issues.'

'From Pisa?' I knew the University of Pisa was noted for medicine, science and engineering, but hadn't heard it was known for economics as well.

'Now I work from Pisa. But for many years I did research in Brussels.'

'Is that where you learned English?'

'Yes, it was the common language. I learned English at school, but didn't speak it until later.'

'And now what do you do?'

'Now I teach. I'm a sort of jukebox. They put in money, and I sing. I don't do any research at all.'

I laughed. I liked the analogy.

He leant back on his chair and, openly grinning, said, 'Do you always ask so many questions?'

I realised, in that moment, that he'd understood a fundamental aspect of my character: curiosity and the desire to understand. 'It's a Greek trait,' I replied. 'I inherited it from my father.'

'Ah,' he said, 'you have Greek blood. So you're familiar with Mediterranean culture.'

I found myself, quite unexpectedly, telling him about the flashes of 'Greekness' I remembered from my childhood, and Giancarlo appeared quite happy to let me ramble on. In fact, he looked almost fascinated. Perhaps he hadn't met a half-Greek, half-English Australian before.

I was trying to think of something to say that wasn't banal and wasn't a question when my telephone rang. It was deep down in my handbag, and what with the rain and, I admit, a touch of nervous apprehension, I'd forgotten to turn it off.

It was Sam: 'Am I disturbing you?'

'No, no, just having dinner with a friend. What's up?'

'You're going to be a grandmother again – in May.'

'That's wonderful – lovely – I'm really, really pleased.'

'We were wondering whether you could make it for the

birth? It'll probably be another caesarean and it'd be great if you were there.'

'Yes, of course I'll be there. I'll speak to you soon. Bye, and take care.'

'My daughter,' I said to Giancarlo. By now my face was one big smile. 'Another baby. I think I've just gone into the lead.'

'Yes, you have,' he said, 'but what lovely news. Let's drink to the new baby.'

He ordered a bottle of icy dry champagne. 'Here's to new beginnings,' he said.

New beginnings!

He drove me home and kissed me oh so gently on the lips. The offer was there – in the air – but I didn't take it. *Che sara' sara'*, I told myself. All in good time.

I was flying to Sydney from London because the flight was much, much cheaper than from Italy. It would also allow me to catch up with my younger sister, Isobel, who worked in London. My London flight wasn't until late the following afternoon, so I had plenty of time to pack up my things and clean the flat. I also had plenty of time to reflect. Yesterday morning, my plan had been to move back to Sydney and pick up at least some of the threads of my old life.

But the previous evening, the situation had once again changed. Sam wouldn't be going anywhere until well after the birth of the new baby, and she needed me in Ireland in May. I hadn't been there for the first birth, and I wasn't going to miss the second, particularly as it was likely to be another caesarean.

I thought back to my ten years in Cambridge. Life had been so stable, one day more or less following the same pattern as the next. The last eighteen months had been a roller-coaster in comparison, and clearly the ride wasn't over yet.

The previous night I'd had dinner with a man I liked – a man who kept popping up at key moments. Was it intuition, or the triumph of hope over reason, that made me believe something important was going to develop between Giancarlo and me? Well, whatever it was, I decided to back it – I would be coming back to Pisa.

CHAPTER 9

From London to Sydney

I stayed overnight with my younger sister in London. Isobel's a little shorter than me but has the same dark eyes. You can see we're from the same tribe.

The front garden of her terraced house in Islington – previously a pretty garden with pots and lavender bushes – had been asphalted to make space for the cars. 'We were giving the council half our salaries in parking fees,' she explained, 'and the rest was going on parking fines.' Isobel and her husband Andrew, both classical musicians, lived a financially precarious life. Andrew was currently on tour in America.

'Anyway,' she added, 'when would we sit in the garden? We're either working or the weather's foul.'

Theirs was a comfortable marriage; they were good friends and liked each other. That seemed to be the key to their shared happiness.

'So,' she said, the intonation indicating a question.

'So what?' I asked.

'Paul,' she said. 'How did it go?'

At that moment I realised I really had moved on. 'We had a lovely time,' I said. 'We keep in touch – but not much. His firm is moving to Melbourne.'

'You know, it's not that easy living with a man. Lots of people would think your situation with Paul perfect.'

I didn't want to go over this old ground, so I changed the subject. 'There's much more exciting news. You're going to be an aunt again!'

'An Irish aunt or a New Zealand aunt?'

'An Irish aunt,' I said, and we both laughed.

'Wonderful news. Does that mean you'll be coming back?'

'Yes. I'll definitely be here for the baby in May, and then I'll probably stick around for a while.'

'What, for another dose of *La Bella Vita* mixed with Mediterranean schmooze?'

'Well yes, if I can get it. Seriously, though, I know my way round Pisa and I need the income, so it seems a good plan.' I didn't say anything about having met a charming Italian because, firstly, she'd have teased the hell out of me and, secondly, my feeling that there was some potential waiting to be explored with Giancarlo wasn't based on anything tangible.

Isobel opened a bottle of French red as I filled her in on Matthew and Rachel in Christchurch, now both studying at the local university, getting top marks and liking university life. We talked about our older sister, Caroline, who'd set up her own business and then moved to the Canary Islands off the coast of North Africa to escape the damp, chilly English climate.

I told Isobel of my short-term plans: to stay initially with Jane and Brian, pay a visit to Françoise, and then spend some time in New Zealand.

'I've got so much to do in Sydney – all those hundred and one things you don't do when you're away: dentist, tax return, stuff to sort out with the flat. And I'll have to get a temporary job. When the tenant moves out I'll be up for the mortgage.'

'You need a rich man!' she said, topping up our glasses.

'So do you!' I replied.

The one bottle of wine became two, and the next day I had a headache as well as the prospect of a twenty-two hour flight. Oh well, I thought, serves me right. I bent down to lift my suitcase. Click, went my back. 'Christ,' I said, tears of pain coming to my eyes, 'I've put my back out.'

'Oh no!' said Isobel. She filled me with painkillers and anti-inflammatories and called a minicab to take me to the airport.

The driver didn't appear to notice my indisposition. He didn't say anything except that he came from Iran. I got the impression that it was all he could say in English, but he smiled a lot. I tried not to think of the journey in front of me.

At the check-in desk I said: 'I've never asked for an upgrade before, and I'm not in the habit of begging, but I've just put my back out. Please, please, please could you upgrade me?'

The check-in attendant – hair scraped back and little pearl ear studs – was sweet, all sympathy and kindness. 'No,' she said, 'sorry, sorry, sorry – no upgrade.'

The next twenty-two hours passed in a painkiller-induced haze.

My dear friend Jane was at the airport to meet me. I threw my arms round her.

'About time you turned up again,' she said, and then: 'You're very pale – and you're limping. What's happened?'

'There wasn't a seat,' I said. 'I had to sit on the pilot's lap.' And as an afterthought: 'He can't walk any straighter than me.'

'Oooh,' she laughed, 'things haven't changed.'

We crossed slowly from the terminal to the carpark. I was so relieved to be on firm ground in Sydney, even if I couldn't remember how I'd got there.

We drove up to the house where I'd spent two years as part of her family, and I realised how lucky I was to have such solid friends.

It was like the old days. Jane and I sat at the kitchen table, falling over our words in an attempt to catch up with all the news, stopping only to refill our cups of tea. We talked about children and grandchildren and the pleasures and trials of living in Italy. We laughed and teased each other and exchanged exaggerated congratulations on how well we were ageing. The letters we'd sent, I knew, had been the bones. Now we were filling in the muscles, tissue and nerves.

A couple of days later, when I was over the jetlag, Jane lent me her car to visit Françoise at the home she had shared with my father for fifteen years. It was sad and moving for both of us. 'I miss him so much,' she said. 'I haven't slept properly since he died. It all seems so empty.'

Françoise's greatest asset, apart from doe-like eyes and thick blonde hair, was the trace of a distinctive and charming French accent.

We sat at the picture window which looked over the garden with its late spring profusion of lemon trees, cream-and-yellow frangipanis and flowering shrubs. 'You weren't here,' she continued. 'You've no idea how difficult it's been.' I asked her to tell me about it, and she described a short stay in hospital, an unexpected heart attack, a gathering of friends to celebrate what had been a long and colourful life, followed by – for her – a terrible vacuum.

'And where is he now?' I asked.

'His body went for research,' she said.

'Yes I know, but where exactly?'

She bristled: 'What does it matter? He's dead.'

I left it. I didn't want to upset her, and anyway I could find out for myself.

I drove back to Jane and Brian's, thinking about what Françoise had said. When I arrived, I got the telephone directory and looked up all the possible teaching hospitals. The calls went like this: 'Have you by any chance received the body of Enricos Kolios who died on 20 February 2000?

The question was met with stunned silence. Clearly they weren't used to dealing in mislaid bodies. 'And what connection do you have to the deceased?'

'Daughter.'

'I see.' You could hear them thinking, good grief – what sort of daughter loses her own father's body?

The first two calls got negative responses. The third call, to a professor of forensic medicine, hit the target: 'Yes,' said the perfectly charming woman, they'd received his body, and if she could help in any way – a visit to the department, perhaps,

161

or a session with a counsellor – she'd be happy to arrange it for me. I declined her offers, but said I wanted to know what had happened to his body. She said that they used their own undertaker, but she would investigate and ring me back.

'So,' I asked, curiosity getting the better of me, 'who paid for the services of the undertaker?'

'We did,' she said. 'It's our way of saying thank you for the donation.'

Donation? Saying thank you? She made it sound like winning a meat tray at the local leagues club.

Later the phone rang. It was a man with a deep, fruity voice, oozing sympathy. I knew this was an undertaker. He couldn't have been anything else. My father, he told me, had been cremated, and his ashes were available for collection.

'But where are you?' I asked.

He named a suburb at least an hour's drive away.

'Is there any possibility of delivery?'

Not by his company, he said, but he could arrange to send the container by post.

And so it was, two days later, that I took my pretty patterned Liberty tote bag up to the local post office, and in return for twelve dollars and seven cents cash-on-delivery, collected what remained of my funny, generous rogue of a father.

'Birthday present, is it?' enquired the clerk.

'Not exactly,' I replied.

I took him to a local outdoor restaurant, sat him on a seat next to me in the shade, and drank to the good times we'd had together.

And where is he now? In Jane and Brian's garden, waiting for the time when, according to the dictates of Greek custom, he can be taken back to his home village in the Olympus mountains. I can imagine the look of amusement and disbelief on his face at the sight of his three daughters standing in a dusty Greek village throwing handfuls of ashes to the wind while bemused village women dressed in black look on.

A week later I moved back into my own flat. To begin with it felt strange to be in the place that had launched me into a new phase of life. The sights and sounds were the same, but I wasn't. Italy had changed me. I found inner city life jarred. It was like an ant heap – everyone scurrying around in their own little bubble, racing to work, restaurants and the gym. I'd grown away from 'yuppie' values and had also come to appreciate a calmer, more human scale of existence. Perhaps, to be fair, I'd have made more effort and seen things in a different light if my return to Sydney had been permanent. But I was here only for a few months, and had exciting things waiting for me on the other side of the world.

I looked for a freelance teaching job in a language school near my flat. I made a couple of telephone calls and was called straight back for an interview. I soon realised why. Not only was the teaching hard work, it was also unrewarding. I'd become spoiled in Italy, with friendly and gracious students. This was like a cattle market with hundreds of students and every classroom crammed full. Students arrived at any point in the course and left at any point, destroying continuity. And worst of all, the school acted as a training college for aspiring teachers of English, so often there would be a trainee teacher, idealistic and unrealistic, watching every move I made.

I spent Christmas with Jane and Brian. We took a hamper to the beach and sat in the shade watching families playing games or splashing in the surf. 'You know,' I mused to Jane as we sat sipping glasses of champagne straight from the Esky, 'there are aspects of life here that I love, but the lifestyle in Italy also has a lot to offer.'

'Well,' she replied, 'your roots are European, so it would be surprising if you didn't feel the connection. Italy is, after all, quite similar to Greece. Why not spend time in both Australia and Italy?'

It sounded like brilliant idea, but not very practicable.

On New Year's Day there was a short email from Giancarlo: *'Buon Anno,'* he wished me.

'Buon Anno anche a te,' I replied. Viewed from Sydney, both Pisa and Giancarlo seemed a very long way away.

By mid-April I'd worked the agreed six months at the language school, and with more than a little relief I passed my flat over to an agent, and flew off to visit Matthew and Rachel in New Zealand. If you drilled a hole from Pisa, and kept drilling straight down, you'd eventually arrive in Christchurch. Like Pisa it's flat, surrounded by mountains and near the sea. But there the similarities end. There's little in the way of elegant dressing or stylish restaurants, and absolutely no drinkable coffee. But what it lacks in sophistication is more than compensated for by the friendliness and good humour of its people.

Matthew and Rachel met me at the airport complete with a bunch of roses from the garden, and then we drove through the leafy suburbs of Christchurch until we reached the large single-storey house where they rented the back half.

I was relieved when Matthew and Rachel settled down to study, because for years they'd travelled the world together, living from hand to mouth. I'd jokingly reminded them that they needed to earn lots of money to keep me in my old age. But the real reason for my anxiety was fear that something would happen to them in some faraway place. On one occasion they were in Indonesia when there was an earthquake. I'd paced the floor for a day before a kind man at the Australian Embassy assured me that their names weren't on the missing list.

They'd bought a dog – a great, slobbering, chocolate-brown labrador. 'We don't want children,' Matthew told me baldly, 'so we've got a dog instead.'

I looked at the dog – playful and stupid. Would I be crotcheting little bed covers for him and making him a cake in the shape of a '2'? I couldn't see it.

Gus the dog had a smart new kennel in the backyard which I admired. 'Pleased you like it,' said Matthew. 'We were thinking it could double up as your retirement home.'

While they were at uni, I took my new 'grandson' for walks round the flat green parks of Christchurch in the crisp autumn air, and thought about the decision not to have children. Matthew was four when my marriage broke up, and he – like me – had effectively grown up without a father. It must have been hard for him with no male role model in his youth. Perhaps that had some bearing on their decision? I would never know, however, because it wasn't the sort of question I felt I could ask.

At the end of April it was time to return to Europe. I found myself with two jam-packed suitcases: one for Ireland, full of toys and cheerful New Zealand wool clothes for Hannah and the new baby, the second with my things and a full length navy-blue waterproof with a stylish hood that Rachel had declared 'cool'. This was a difficult moment for me. I didn't like living so far away from Matthew and Rachel and never knowing when I would see them again. My years at boarding school had left me with a sort of stoicism – to accept what I couldn't change – but as they drove me to the airport, I felt a tingly sensation which meant tears weren't far behind. By the time I'd paid my departure tax and passed through the gate, I was in full flood.

I arrived in Northern Ireland a day and a half later. Although it was now May – springtime – Ireland seemed greyer and damper than ever. Sam, hugely pregnant and a little apprehensive, was booked in for a caesarean in two days' time. When she left for the hospital, it was like the old days in Cambridge when she was a schoolgirl, with me kissing her goodbye and encouraging her to do well. I fought back a tear . . . your children, no matter how old they are, are always your children, and whatever they go through, part of you always goes through it with them.

It was another girl – Ellie – a perfect little thing with large dark eyes and long, long limbs. 'She looks like you,' everyone told me. I thought so too.

The days dissolved one into the next. We started early – and continued all day doing the tasks that must be done when you have a baby and a toddler – until we collapsed exhausted, only to do it all again the next day. I'd forgotten what it was like. No wonder new mothers get depressed, I thought, and no wonder Sam wanted me to help.

I took the baby for walks, bathed her and changed her nappies. She calmed down when I took her in my arms and rocked her, and as I peered into her huge eyes I felt nothing but love. Babies can do that to you.

But of course she wasn't my baby, and after a few weeks, it was time for me to start thinking about organising my own life.

I rang Jim, the Director of Studies, in Pisa: 'It's me again!'

'Thank goodness!' he exclaimed. 'Everyone's leaving town and we're desperate for people to teach the July and September courses.'

I agreed to do both. It was, again, a good arrangement for me: two months in Italy with a month in Ireland in between.

I emailed Sarah to ask her if she knew of any spare accommodation. Surely someone who was away would be happy to sublet for a couple of months? Sarah emailed back that there was a student house close to the school, and as most university exams had finished, there would almost certainly be a room free.

I telephoned the signora and booked a room for July and September. The rent was 400,000 lire a month – less than I'd paid before – and it included bills.

I sent a brief email to Giancarlo to let him know that I

would be arriving in July, and hoped to see him. In his return message he said he was happy to hear of my return, but he had exams to conduct at that time and was then going straight to Sardinia with friends. He wouldn't be around until September.

I felt a flash of disappointment. Although we'd had only one brief communication in the last six months, I'd been hoping for more. Had my intuition been wrong? Was I deluding myself? Calm down, I thought, it's just a question of timing. Be patient.

I took the early morning flight from Belfast, once again looking down on the Alps and wondering what lay ahead. Only this time, my thoughts were more practical. I had courses starting the following afternoon, which gave me only one day to prepare the lessons and settle in to my new lodgings.

The four-storey house of Signora Bucheri stood on the corner of a small, rectangular piazza. It had recently been painted a sandy yellow and, with the Tuscan green shutters, it looked very smart. The other buildings round the piazza were shops with apartments above, and a medieval church which sat incongruously next to the multiscreen cinema. In view behind the square were the imposing law courts, and the turn-of-the-century porticoed Teatro Verdi. The house was a two-minute walk from the school and town centre.

The attractive wrapping, however, did not reflect the contents. The entrance hall gave way to two flights of dark stairs with peeling paint and crumbling brickwork. The signora explained that she lived on the first floor, the students

– all girls – lived on the second, and her son and his wife on the third. Her daughter-in-law was a foreigner, she told me with a grimace.

The signora spoke slowly, but with an accent that sounded perhaps Russian. She was in her sixties and short – under five foot – but what she lacked in height was more than made up for in girth. She had tinted chestnut hair, and one of those floral cotton housecoats that reminded me of war-time films.

I was the only tenant at the moment, she told me. However, as compensation, she was giving me a large corner room which normally served as a double rather than single. I would have to move when the students returned.

The apartment had seven bed-sits, two bathrooms and a large kitchen. The furniture was old but functional. As the signora showed me around I noticed missing lampshades, cracked tiles and general shabbiness. What did she do with the rent money? It certainly wasn't going on maintaining the flat.

The next morning I called in to the school to collect my timetable and plan the afternoon lessons. There, in the little lane outside the school, chained up exactly where I had left it some nine months earlier, was a very dirty *cavallo verde*, – my faithful green bicycle. I imagined it would have been stolen or cleared away by the council, but no, there it stood, tyres completely flat, like the most loyal of servants waiting for its master. I would collect it later. Now I had to concentrate on work.

'Hello,' said Tom, and paused. He seemed lost for words. 'Ahem . . . yes . . . welcome, welcome. Did you have a good trip? Jolly good. Now, we've got three classes for you. I think you'll find them interesting.'

The first was a group of students taking an advanced Cambridge exam in December. They were halfway through the course, and couldn't afford to take the usual three-month summer break. I recognised the name of one of the students. He'd been in my class of teenagers two years earlier and had been the only failure. He was a nice boy . . . well, if you count bone idle as nice. He certainly wasn't a problem – just a failure.

The second group consisted of two girls doing another Cambridge exam. Both of them had taken the exam before and failed. There was just one student in the third class, in her second year, and by now I could guess that she, too, had failed her exam. What was going on? Why was I getting landed with all the failures? I went to ask Jim.

'Well,' he said, grinning, 'it's your fault. The word's gone round about your Trinity College students who all got distinctions. Everyone wants you because they think you'll get them through the exams.'

'I haven't got a magic wand,' I protested. 'And you know as well as I do that they should have been entered at a higher level.'

'Yes, I know,' he said, 'but Tom insisted. Student numbers are down and he wants everyone to be happy with their teacher.'

And what about the teacher? I thought. But I didn't say anything. I'd learned how things worked both in the school and in the country. When it's clear that you're going to get shafted, you smile sweetly, say nothing, and then work your way round it later. Everyone knows what you're up to, of course, but as long as you don't tackle anything head-on, it's acceptable.

The range of excuses and evasions is enormous, and I've concluded that the cunning which underpins many inter-actions in Italy also gives Italians a quick-wittedness and *savoir faire* which for foreigners can be beguiling. It can also be unbelievable. I recall seeing a television interview with a politician who had responsibility for overseeing the construc-tion of a new reservoir. It seemed that the reservoir, which was in an isolated part of southern Italy, appeared on the maps but didn't, in fact, exist; neither did the millions of lire the government had provided to pay for it. You'd think he'd be dead meat, but no. He calmly explained that the plans had undergone some changes, and there had been difficulties with the site and with the contractors. One implausible excuse followed the other until, at the end of a frustrating half-hour, the interviewer finally asked: 'Look, is there a reser-voir or isn't there?'

The politician smiled slowly and winningly: 'I've explained the position to you. What do I have to do now – bring the reservoir into the studio?'

He'd won. Doubtless there would be ramifications behind the scenes, but the Italian public was left with the impression that he was just trying to do his job against enormous odds. The people's sympathy went out to him because they could identify with his frustrations, and they didn't give a damn whether there was a reservoir or not.

I called Sarah: 'Hi, I'm back!'

'Brilliant,' she said. 'There's a *sagra* tonight at Vicopisano. Why don't we go together?'

Vicopisano is a picturesque fortified hill town with wonderful views over the plains near Pontedera, east of Pisa. Being high up, it would almost certainly offer a cool breeze – a welcome relief from the fierce July heat. *Sagra* comes from the word 'sacred', and is a festival to celebrate a local harvest, such as grapes, wild boar or olives depending on the season. The *sagra* at Vicopisano was to celebrate the tomato harvest, so we could expect lots of bruschetta (toasted bread topped with chopped fresh tomato, basil and oil) and rich tomato-based pasta sauces.

Sagras are held from early summer through to autumn, and as well as good food, they offer *ballo liscio*. *Ballo liscio* (literally 'smooth dance'), is old-time dancing under the stars to a live orchestra. People of all ages and from all backgrounds crowd onto the wooden floor, dancing waltzes and foxtrots under the trees in the cool night air. Most couples dance very well, and I was reminded that dancing was in the past one of the few acceptable ways that the men could lay their hands on the women. No wonder they were all so good at it.

Sarah picked me up outside Pontedera station and as we drove along we exchanged news . . . she had met someone, she told me: 'One of my students. He asked me out to dinner, and we've been seeing each other ever since. He's lovely, but he works in Milan.'

'Is that a problem?' I asked.

'Not at the moment. Anyway, we'll see – it's early days. While we're on the subject, have you heard from Giancarlo?'

'We exchanged New Year's greetings, but that's all. He probably didn't believe I'd come back. Anyway, I let him know I was here, but he's tied up until September.'

'That's reasonable. You can't expect him to sit around waiting for you to turn up.'

Sarah was right. 'Anyway,' I said with a grin, doing my best to imitate her tone: 'we'll see – it's early days.'

At the *sagra* we found ourselves a table fronting the dance floor and ordered our food – pasta with sardines, tomato and pine nuts – together with a bottle of local red wine. Later, feeling mellow and relaxed after the wine and food, we accepted offers to dance under the stars with men who were half my age and half my height.

The lessons, however, weren't going as smoothly as the *ballo liscio*. The five students doing the advanced Cambridge exam were fed up. They felt they were being mucked around. They'd already had two teachers – I was the third – and with the exam looming in December, they had covered less than half the course work. It's unusual for Italians to be so out-spoken, but I understood why. They'd paid a lot of money for the course, which included the entrance fee for the exam, and were pessimistic about their chances of passing. No teacher likes taking over a class under such circumstances. There was only one thing to do: I worked them hard. I gave them verbs and constructions to learn, set extra homework and lent them tapes to listen to at home. It meant more work for me, but at least it gave the students a chance of passing the exam.

Rino, in his thirties with dark curly hair and a beard, had been in Bosnia with the UN peacekeeping forces. Intelligence, humour and sheer goodness radiated from him. So did some of the worst *parolacce* (swearwords) I'd ever heard. 'Okay, Rino,' I would say, 'what do you do with question number five?'

'How the fuck would I know?' he'd say in Italian. 'Shove it up your arse, most like!'

The women tittered and then pretended not to have heard. Matteo grinned from one lazy ear to the other.

'Eh, eh,' I chided, 'that's enough. It's quite simple. You have to put it in reported speech, so go back a tense and then change the adverbs.'

'Well why in Christ's name didn't you say so before?' His face broke into another huge smile as he tipped his chair back in satisfaction.

The others adored Rino, none more so than Donatella. She was in her forties and, unusually for an Italian woman, wore no makeup and favoured sensible rather than elegant clothes. She engineered to sit next to him, and they did all their pair work together. 'You know,' she said one evening as she was leaving the classroom, 'I love Rino because he is completely himself and doesn't modify his behaviour just because I'm a nun.'

A what? All that filth was being absorbed by a bride of Christ? I was appalled. I felt it was a reflection on me, that I had allowed such language in my classroom. She saw my expression: 'Ah,' she said, 'you didn't know. Well, I hope you won't spoil anything for me.'

As well as a dirty mouth, Rino had a strange surname: Sconosciuto, which means 'unknown'. He explained, in his own florid way, that it was a euphemism for 'illegitimate'. Centuries ago, babies born out of wedlock were abandoned at the convent gates. They were taken in, and all given the same surname.

I couldn't resist it. 'I knew it,' I said, 'you're just one big bastard!'

He leaned back on his chair again and grinned.

July was coming to an end. I was off to spend August in Ireland, and Sarah was going to teach in a summer school in Oxford. We planned one last outing before we left. 'One of my students,' Sarah told me, 'runs an *agriturismo* just outside Pontedera and he's invited me to come for the day and bring a friend.' I had no idea what an *agriturismo* was, but she just said mysteriously, 'Bring your swimming things and suntan lotion.'

As usual, I got the train from Pisa to Pontedera, and as Sarah's little blue car whizzed round the corner and pulled up outside the station, I felt a surge of excitement. Whatever an *agriturismo* turned out to be, I was sure we were in for a lovely day together. We drove through the rolling hills dotted with cypress trees and ancient stone farmhouses, turned into a little lane and wound our way up into the hills. At the end of the road was a sign which read 'Agriturismo Niccolai'.

As I was to discover, an *agriturismo* is an establishment that falls somewhere between a farm, restaurant, modest hotel and health resort. They are subsidised by the government to encourage both tourism and the cultivation of local produce. The oil, wine, olives, meat and vegetables all come directly from the *agriturismo*. You can stay at reasonable cost, or simply visit for lunch or dinner. It's a perfect way to appreciate Italian rural life.

This one turned out to be extremely popular. We stood in the doorway of the crowded dining room looking round at the large, noisy family groups. Immediately Sarah spotted her student, Massimo the owner, who gestured us towards a table for two at the window looking out over the fields. There was no menu. Or rather, there was a fixed menu, which by now I recognised as a typical Sunday Tuscan lunch: an antipasto of sliced cold meats with olives and other vegetables *sotto olio* (preserved in olive oil). Then a pasta with meat sauce – *spaghetti al ragu* – followed by *involtini*: thin slices of rolled beef and ham flavoured with rosemary, with a salad. The final course was peaches and watermelon, cheese and Sarah's favourite *cantuccini* and *vin santo*.

The courses came slowly, giving us lots of time to appreciate the local red wine and talk. We gossiped about work, and then, thinking of my own feelings of being torn in two every time I leave my family, I asked: 'Do you miss Brisbane?'

She sighed. 'Yes and no. I miss my family and I wish they were closer, particularly my mum, but I've been away a long time. Most of my friends have moved on, and after a few weeks in Brisbane . . . well, I start missing Italy.'

I knew what she meant. Or at least I thought I did. Italy has the allure of 'the other'. It gets under your skin in a way you don't realise until you leave.

We finished lunch and went for a stroll through the olive grove to the swimming pool. The only difficulty was finding the will to move, but with a bit of effort we eventually made it, slumped into the lounge chairs under a cool canvas umbrella and both fell fast asleep.

CHAPTER 10

From Ireland to Pisa – and Giancarlo

It goes without saying that Northern Ireland doesn't share many aspects of an Italian *agriturismo*, but the long, slow summer twilights had a strange, haunting beauty. And somehow this year the air seemed clearer and less redolent of the farmyard. But I wasn't here as a tourist, I was here to see the babies and be with Sam.

'Come on,' I said to Hannah, 'let's put your sister in the pram and go and have afternoon tea together.'

We walked to the centre of town and she indicated the tea-rooms that she favoured: 'We go there 'cos I like the scones.'

Right. I ordered scones and a cappuccino for me. I watched mesmerised as the girl put a teaspoonful of instant coffee into a mug, followed by hot milk, and then inverted one of those small lunar space capsules and with a schlerping sound sprayed the top with a mountain of synthetic cream. Later, as we prepared to leave, Hannah said in the penetrating high-pitched voice of an almost three-year-old, 'Granny, why haven't you drunk your coffee?'

My daughter told me that their application to Australia had met with some difficulties. It was going to take longer than they thought – at least another year. 'Well,' I said, 'I'm sorry, because I know you're anxious to go and a year's a long time when you're waiting for something to happen.'

Later that evening, I lay in bed – where I do most of my thinking – and considered the latest development. The delay felt like fate playing into my hands. I had – strangely – come to believe that Giancarlo was going to be part of my life story. Now I could find out, and still be close to Sam and the grand-children.

Like the previous year, we celebrated my birthday and the following week I made a birthday cake for Hannah – this year shaped like a '3' – and topped with Barbie in her holiday outfit: checked top, pink cotton trousers and high-heeled sandals that only a deformed plastic doll could wear. I thought back to my own childhood. My mother wouldn't have allowed Barbie in the house, let alone stuck on a cake. I pulled myself up – I'd sworn I'd never begin any sentence with 'When I was young . . .'

August bled into September, and it was time to leave. 'Bye-bye, babies,' I said, hugging them tightly, 'I'll see you at Christmas.'

'Oh, Granny,' said Hannah, '*I'm* not a baby!'

My mobile phone rang as the No. 3 bus swung round the corner where Giardino Scotto meets the Arno on the ten-minute ride from the airport.

It was Giancarlo: 'Ah, you're back!' he exclaimed.

'Well, almost.'

'Would you be free for lunch later this week? I'll ring you nearer the time.'

Italians often call you to tell you when they will call you again. I usually find it bemusing, but on this occasion I was delighted. Giancarlo had remembered the date of my return and had – true to his word – rung me. I smiled to myself. My intuition, it seemed, was in good working order. His next call was something to look forward to in the busy week ahead. In the meantime, I had lessons to prepare and work to do.

Gea and Stephania, the two girls Tom had insisted on giving me back in July, were both hardworking university students and I couldn't understand why they'd failed the Cambridge exam. So I decided to watch the way they studied in class to see if I could spot anything. I soon discovered the problem. Every time I gave them a piece of writing, they reached for their coloured markers. Instead of absorbing English in a natural way, they were analysing it to death. But language – at least spoken language – isn't like that. It's intu-itive, it's responsive – it comes from the heart not the head.

'Okay, no coloured pens today,' I said firmly.

They looked anxious. 'But how will we remember things?'

'It doesn't matter if you don't remember.'

They didn't look convinced.

We did yoga breathing exercises and guided visualisations. They thought I'd gone mad. 'Close your eyes,' I said, 'and imagine you're walking on the beach. Describe everything – every little detail: what you are wearing, what you can see. Where is the sun? Feel the sand, the sea . . . describe it all.'

Gea began first, but fell silent after two or three sentences.

I persisted. Every lesson, we did basic yoga exercises, humming, listening to songs and absolutely no colouring-in. As the girls relaxed into it, the lessons became more fun for all of us and their speaking improved.

Giancarlo rang on Wednesday: 'What are your plans?' he asked.

'Well, today I'm teaching, but tomorrow I'm free.'

'Good,' he said. 'How about lunch? Where can I pick you up?'

We arranged to meet at the church on the corner of Via San Francesco and Via Donati, two minutes from my flat, at one o'clock sharp.

Italians, surprisingly, are extremely punctual: it's just that their concept of timekeeping is rather different from ours. If it's important to be on time (for a train or bus), or if it would be considered impolite to be late (for a lesson or doctor's appointment), they are punctilious. If, however, it's an arrangement to go to the beach or for a coffee, they are beyond casual. They'll turn up an hour late, ring at the last minute to say they're not coming, or offer an excuse that is an embarrassingly obvious lie.

I rang Sarah: 'Guess who's invited me to lunch?'

'Well, well . . . Relax, have a great time. Let him do everything for you. Italian men love looking after their women – at least at the beginning,' and she laughed.

In the meantime, I was facing another difficult situation at work. I cursed Tom. This was the third 'hard case' he'd given me, and this one really did push me to the limit. Silvia was a *rompi palle*, which means 'ball-breaker', and is used to describe a certain type of woman who is overconfident, spoiled, and doesn't know where to draw the line. In polite usage it is modified to *rompi scatole* (cardboard box breaker) but everyone knows what it really means. Silvia was a fine example.

She flounced into the first lesson fifteen minutes late, all gushing energy. She didn't look at me, just threw her Gucci bag on the desk and said, 'Sorry, oooh, so sorry I'm late. I had to collect my shoes from the shoe mender and then I found I'd left my purse at home, and then . . .' All this in Italian at a hundred miles an hour. She was in her twenties, attractive, with streaked blonde hair and Prada shoes. Money oozed out of every pore.

She hadn't failed her Level 2 exam, she told me, but rather hadn't liked her teacher, had stopped coming to class and had then asked for individual lessons in compensation. I found out later that the teacher in question had asked her to be removed from his class because of her rudeness and disruptive effect on the other students. She questioned everything I said, often flatly contradicting me. She obviously thought that because she'd paid for the lessons, and because

Tom was a friend of her father's, she could get away with anything.

I fell back on the tactics that I'd employed with *rompi palle* students in my high school teaching days. I wrote out a list of conditions, one for her, one for me. At the next lesson I said with a big and totally false smile: 'You know, Silvia, because of your previous bad experience, I'm really anxious that you get the most from these lessons. I've drawn up some guidelines so you can really profit from our time together.'

The first condition was that if she was more than ten minutes late, the lesson would be cancelled. The second was that she bring her books to class. The third was that she turn off her mobile phone during the lessons, and the fourth was that she do her homework. Her eyes narrowed. She wasn't used to being challenged, and although I'd presented it in a positive way, she knew the message was: Buckle under, sister, or you're out.

I never referred to the list again. We both knew what the game was: she could either back down and behave normally, or continue to play on her connection with Tom and ignore me. However, being asked to leave two classes could prove embarrassing. Not for her – she didn't give a damn – but for her family. I was counting on this. If I was wrong, things could get a lot worse. For now, I just had to wait and hope for the best.

Thursday was bright and sunny. I hadn't seen Giancarlo for nearly a year, and as I got out a simple dark blue dress, gold earrings and bracelet, I realised how much I was looking forward to seeing him again. Just before one o'clock I added a splash of Chanel No 19 and began the short walk to the church where we'd arranged to meet. There in the street was Giancarlo, walking towards me: same big smile, open face with warm Latin eyes, and hands extended in greeting. 'Hello, hello,' he beamed. 'Welcome back. You look well.'

It was so easy, so natural. We turned towards the car. I, momentarily forgetting that everything in an Italian car is reversed, made for the driver's door. He smiled and said: 'You're perfectly welcome to drive, but you may be more comfortable in the passenger seat.'

With a smile to match his, I countered, 'And why exactly *do* Italians drive on the wrong side of the road?'

We drove to Marina di Pisa, to a restaurant on stilts built into the rocks overlooking the sea where Lisa and I had bathed last summer. Giancarlo pointed out the islands, three faint grey soufflés rising on the horizon: Elba, where Napoleon was imprisoned, Capraia and Gorgona, the latter now a prison colony holding some of Italy's most notorious criminals.

We ordered seafood with *vernaccia* – the crisp, dry white wine from San Gimignano – chatted on in the Anglo–Italian style that I'd become so familiar with. I described the events of the past year, and he nodded, his eyes fixed on mine. It felt natural telling him about my life, as if he was a close friend and already knew the people and places concerned. He stopped me every so often with a comment or a question: what did I think of Christchurch? Did Hannah like her new sister?

The waiter arrived with plates of whitebait and other

seafood fried to a light golden crispness. As we ate he told me about Sardinia: 'I go there most summers for a week or two. I have friends with a villa in an isolated area in the west.' He grinned: 'It's great because there are no foreigners.'

'I know what you mean,' I said solemnly. 'Foreigners can be a real pain.'

'Yes,' he agreed, looking at me with laughter round his eyes, 'and no. Anyway, we swam and played a game or two of tennis, but mostly we took the boat out. Do you like sailing?'

'I love sailing, it's just that it doesn't much like me. Recently I've started getting seasick.'

'Patches,' he said. 'You need patches. They're excellent – we've all got them.'

What did he mean? Eye patches like Long John Silver?

'What *sort* of patches?' I asked.

'Little skin patches. They stop you being sick.'

He told me he'd sailed to most parts of the Mediterranean, but the really fascinating places were to be found on the coast of North Africa. While he was speaking, he leant forward and touched my hand, just as he had at our dinner at Torre del Lago. But this time he didn't pull his hand away.

As we strolled along the seafront after lunch he invited me to see a new exhibition of modern art in Pisa. We drove home, and he dropped me off on the corner of the piazza outside the house:

'Thank you for lunch,' I said, as we stood together by the car.

'Thank you for coming back,' he replied, gently pulling me towards him.

At this point the car behind us started tooting in an insistent, truly Italian way. I looked round: we were blocking his path.

The other tenants would soon be arriving at the flat for the beginning of term. I had to decide what to do about accommodation. Most flats and rooms in Pisa get passed around by word of mouth and are never advertised. I was reasonably comfortable where I was – it was cheap and convenient – and sharing with Italians would certainly improve my Italian and understanding of their culture. I had my own room to escape to, and my earplugs for sleeping. I'd think of it as an adventure, and if it got too much, I'd find somewhere else. I asked Signora Bucheri if I could stay on. She was pleased. I was quiet and might, perhaps, have a good influence on the others, who were all students. I would, however, have to swap rooms.

The first of them, Antonella, arrived from Sardinia with her mother and a suitcase full of food. Her mother went out straight away and bought mops, buckets and industrial quantities of cleaning products (which were already supplied) and cleaned and scrubbed the flat from top to bottom.

Ilaria and Tiziana from San Remo arrived next. They were sharing the double room. In tow were their mothers, with the tuckboxes and disinfectant. Katia, a school friend of theirs from San Remo, moved in the following day and yes, there again was mother in serious cleaning mode.

A couple of days later Michela arrived from Grosseto, a

town further south in Tuscany. She was studying literature, and this was her fourth year at both university and the flat. She'd spent six months in Ireland and spoke English well. Michela was the one I had most in common with; she also didn't come with a cleaning-obsessed mother.

A week later Maria, together with her mother, father, brother and boyfriend, arrived from Calabria in the deep south of Italy. I had heard comments about the differences between southerners and northerners, but this was my first look at southerners close up. Maria was beautiful – really gorgeous in that sultry, sexy, Latin way. She walked like a model, hips swinging and one foot directly in the front of the other. The boyfriend, to my eye, looked a bit *ghiozzo* (rough), but that didn't matter because Maria's mother never left them alone together for a minute. They all went out to do the obligatory shopping, returning with bags and bags of provisions, and then the fun began.

During lunch, the kitchen door burst open, and there – dressed in black like an apparition from hell – stood the mother. Why, she demanded, should Maria have the cupboard space furthest away from the stove? It would be very inconvenient for her when she was cooking. Someone would have to swap.

There was a stunned silence. I thought I hadn't understood so I kept quiet.

Katia, a sensible girl, said calmly: 'Well, there are seven cupboards and seven people. We've all chosen ours, and as Maria was the last to arrive she takes what's left.'

The mother turned on her. 'What?' she shouted. 'You

expect me to accept that? We pay more rent for Maria's room' – which was true, she had the largest single room with a view over the square – 'and that includes kitchen space!'

All the while Maria was cowering behind her mother's back. She obviously didn't like it, but what could she do? I guessed from her expression that she was used to these scenes.

Her mother stormed off to Signora Bucheri, who – looking weary but compliant – came up and said: '*Per carita* [for heaven's sake], someone change cupboards with Maria. Her mother's completely mad.'

Later the girls told me that the mamma had demonstrated *una brutta figura* – a bad show. Illaria, more outspoken than the others, described it as *una figura di merda* (literally 'a show like shit'). Examples of *brutta figura* are being loud and vulgar in company, getting drunk in public, going into a bar and using the toilet without buying a drink, which in Italy is tantamount to going into someone's home and using their bathroom without speaking to them – the exact opposite of *bella figura*. I felt sorry for Maria. She was never well accepted after that, the sins of the mother being visited – unfairly – on the daughter. She was also, perhaps, a touch too beautiful.

All of the girls were pleasant and friendly to me. They asked me about Australia, were intrigued that I drank tea in preference to coffee, and couldn't understand why my mobile phone didn't ring all the time.

I was beginning to focus a little more on my appearance and decided a good haircut was in order. I had never been to the hairdressers in Pisa, preferring to wait until I was somewhere where they spoke English, so I asked Michela if she knew anywhere good. She hesitated, and then said that she didn't know for sure, but there was a hairdressers a little further along the street – why didn't I try them?

The next morning, I went to see. I pushed open the wooden and glass door of the salon, and was immediately engulfed in a cloud of cigarette smoke. As the door banged shut behind me and the smoke cleared, I could see two women sitting in chairs facing the large mirrors in front of them. One was surely one of the witches from Macbeth. Her unnaturally black hair – long and straggly – shot out from her head at right angles. She was sitting looking at her own apparition in the mirror and puffing on a cigarette.

The other woman, who I now realised was the hairdresser, sat in the chair next to her chatting and also dragging on a fag. I noticed that she not only had a terrible perm, but that the roots of her hair were several shades lighter than the rest of it. The floor was dirty and littered with hair cuttings. The only decorations I could see were vases of cheap, plastic flowers covered in dust. I turned to go.

'Signora,' said the hairdresser, jumping up and clutching my arm. 'Please sit down. I have just the right style for you.' She pushed me onto the chair next to the witch. My nerve failed. What the hell, I thought, it will grow out in time.

The hairdresser, fag in mouth, proceeded to snip and clip at the back of my head. Every time she took a step, she slipped on the residue of lacquer that she'd used to cement the witch's hair: 'Oops,' she'd cry, scissors in hand like a dagger, as yet again she narrowly missed stabbing me in the head.

Finally she'd finished. I have to admit that it was a terrific cut: quite short, but a good shape and modern without being ridiculous. She motioned me over to the handbasin. In the middle of the shampoo, the phone rang. I only heard her side of the conversation, but it was obvious that she was being summoned.

'Excuse me,' she said, 'I have to go. My daughter is sick at school and I have to collect her and take her home.'

'How long will you be?'

'I've no idea, but wait there. I'll be back soon.'

I waited, with damp soapy hair, for fifteen minutes, and then I stuck one of her towels round my head and walked the short distance home to have a hot shower and rinse the shampoo out of my hair. As I glanced behind me, I saw an eerie figure with a vast black halo emerge from the hairdressers, jump into a car and drive off at speed.

That evening, with everyone sitting at the table, I told the story of the hairdresser.

'That's incredible,' said Katia. 'For a start, hairdressers here are usually men, and secondly they're fastidiously clean and careful. But thanks for the warning. Have you taken back the towel and paid?' she asked as an afterthought.

'Not yet. I need a day or two to get over the shock.'

On Saturday, Giancarlo rang. We agreed to meet by the church the following morning, this time on our bikes.

It was a sharp, sunny day, so I decided to go to the flea market. I'd have a *sfoglia* – a layered pastry dusted with icing sugar – and a cappuccino on the way. The bar was warm with the aroma of coffee, and as I ate my pastry, I browsed through the local paper: 'Women have to wait. That is their lot. If men aren't allowed to pursue women, get hungry, get maddened, they won't be committed – they won't have fully made their decision. An indecisive man makes a bad husband.' I read this in the women's page.

At eleven o'clock *in punto* the next morning, Giancarlo and I met outside the church. As we cycled through the narrow lanes and under the arches of the old medieval quarter of the town, I recounted the story of my haircut.

'So you had a . . .' he paused. 'A brush with disaster.'

He did puns, too? 'Perhaps,' I countered, 'it was more . . . a close shave.'

We arrived at the gallery, which was tucked under the porticoes of the old market square. The entrance made it look like a shop, but inside the space opened up into a large hall with whitewashed walls and terracotta tiled floor. The exhibition was strange – pastel shapes and textured images created from lumps of paint. I didn't understand it and I didn't like it. 'You know, I find myself quite traditional when it comes to art,' I ventured.

'Me too,' he said. 'This is crap, isn't it? Shall we have a coffee?'

I needn't have been so polite. Giancarlo clearly didn't mince words.

We cycled to a bar in Piazza Dante and sat outside under the umbrellas and watched mothers with small children feeding the pigeons and older children running around in the morning sunshine. 'What else have you been up to?' he asked, stirring his coffee.

I gave him a quick update, and finished with the story of Maria and her mother.

'That's southerners for you,' he said. 'The women are as hard as nails – and aggressive with it.'

I was momentarily reminded of the antagonism that exists between Sydney and Melbourne. When I visited Melbourne for work, I soon learned to say that I came from Cambridge (which got smiles and words of encouragement) and not Sydney (which usually provoked a diatribe about how up themselves Sydnersiders were).

Rivalry in Italy went on at a local level as well as a regional one. I had, for example, noticed bad feeling between people from Livorno and Pisa. I wondered if it was a historical legacy from the time of competing city-states – or perhaps something more basic like soccer rivalry. I asked Giancarlo.

He smiled. 'It's not a true hatred,' he explained, 'it's more like sibling rivalry. We have the university but little industry, so the Livornese claim we're privileged and stuck up. Livorno is more colourful and cosmopolitan, so we say they're rough and lack sophistication. It's just a harmless game of words.'

Giancarlo looked at his watch. He had to go. Family lunch, he explained. He was in the habit of cooking for his son, daughter-in-law and grandson on Sundays. He cooks for the family!

He leant forward and took my hand. 'Why don't you come for dinner one evening? I'll make something simple.'

I nodded.

He gave my hand a sqeeze and said: 'I'll call you.'

Five days later I was being ushered into Giancarlo's apartment on the top floor of a *palazzo* overlooking the river. The high ceilings and marbled floors gave it an air of graciousness, but through the doors leading off the entrance hall I could see books, photos and general evidence of family life – a sort of friendly confusion.

'I have a cleaning lady,' he said, 'and she does everything. My wife was good in the house, but I'm not really interested.' He was, it seemed, a typical male.

He led me along a corridor with grey-green walls and framed prints of Mediterranean ports, into the kitchen, which looked like a French country kitchen. It had double stone sinks and an old oak dresser full of attractive white china and around the walls on high shelves were the myriad pots and pans that Giancarlo used on the huge gas range. The scrubbed wooden kitchen table had served his family for two generations, he told me. But just one glance through the double windows – the ochre houses, red-tiled roofs with square chimney stacks, and dark green shutters against the mountain backdrop – confirmed that this couldn't be France: it could only be Italy.

'It's a great kitchen,' I said.

'That's good, because we'll be eating here,' he replied. 'I hope you like the food as well.'

He poured us each a glass of wine, then went back to his cooking. He was preparing pasta, bream and salad. He moved quickly from one pot to the next, tasting, checking, adding salt.

'Where did you learn to cook?' I asked as I sipped my wine.

'In Brussels. The canteen food was so disgusting I started cooking for myself, and ended up feeding all the other

Italians. When my wife was ill I started to cook at home. And now my daughter-in-law is very busy – she works and has the child to look after – so I make Sunday lunch for us all.' Then he smiled and said: 'Actually, the pretence is that they come to visit me on Sundays, but the truth is that she hates cooking.'

He really is a kind man, I thought. He cooks for them all, and goes along with the idea that it's for his benefit. And, although it was hardly the moment, I thought of Paul and his complete lack of domestic skills.

As we ate, he asked: 'What was it like growing up with divorced parents? It's so rare in Italy – I can't imagine it.'

'Well, I didn't know any different. And I went to boarding school quite young. It probably affected me later. I didn't understand what marriage was. I had no idea at all.'

'I didn't really know either,' he said, 'but I was nearly thirty and all my friends were getting married. I guess I just didn't want to be left out.'

We talked and talked, and when it was time to go, he said: 'You could always stay . . .' He ran his hand across my shoulder and gently turned my face towards him as he spoke, his movements a confirmation of what we both wanted. He kissed me, and pulled me towards him. 'Come on,' he said gently, taking my hand and leading me into the bedroom.

I started to get undressed, and all the while he was holding me and helping me. 'I want to look at you,' he whispered. 'I want to touch you. I want everything.' He pulled back the sheet and hurriedly removed his own clothes until we were both lying together, warmed by the heat and desire of each other's body.

I pressed myself into him as he whispered to me in Italian . . . words of love and passion that I understood from the gentle rhythm and stroking of his hands and mouth. I felt his breath on my stomach followed by wetness and heat. He kissed me, flicking his tongue in my mouth and all the while gently caressing me with his hands. Suddenly it welled up, that feeling of completeness and joy, the feeling that had been missing for so long. I held him in my arms and looked at him. In the muted light through the open door he looked younger somehow, and innocent. *'Bella,'* he kept whispering, *'sei bella.'*

That is how my Italian romance really began. I don't know what triggers and mechanisms are at work to attract people, to inexorably pull one to the other, I only know that at a certain point you give in, you stop thinking about it, and you abandon yourself to whatever lies ahead.

The next day Sarah rang: 'How did it go?'

'Perfect,' I said dreamily. 'Absolutely perfect.'

'I'm so pleased. Enjoy it!'

Giancarlo and I started the slow process of really getting to know each other. Like a pass-the-parcel, we unwrapped each layer – carefully, tentatively – to see what came next. And we laughed a lot. I realised that being in tune with someone has to do with how they are, not what language they speak. And being older, paradoxically, we felt we had all the time in the world: time to savour what we had together, and not worry too much about dashing on to something else.

Sometimes Giancarlo would ring during the day: 'Are you free? Shall we go for a drive and lunch?'

It was at one such lunch, in a small trattoria overlooking the river, that I asked him about life at the university.

'Oh,' he said, 'like everything here, it runs on a system of organised chaos.' He went on to describe a situation where all students have the 'democratic right' to go to the university of their choice. Students enrol in their chosen course on the first day of term, and the administration has no way of knowing, except based on past years, how many students will turn up. This leads to the familiar sight of two hundred students crammed into a lecture theatre designed for half that number. The overspill is catered for in the local cinema, which rents its four theatres to the university in the mornings.

It sounded so ridiculous I wanted to laugh. But by now I had heard so many unbelievable stories about how things worked in Italy (and discovered some for myself) that I didn't doubt that what he said was true. And he hadn't finished. The students, he told me, also have the 'democratic right' to take exams when they are ready, and to do them again if they aren't happy with the marks. Retaking exams is common, and in part explains why it takes most Italians five to six years to graduate instead of the usual three or four.

I thought of my own university career all those years ago. Would I have been lining up to retake exams to get better marks? I couldn't imagine it. But then there have always been jobs in Australia. In Italy, there is little work available, and jobs tend to get passed around by people in the know. One of the few ways to break in for people without contacts is to have a brilliant university degree, even if it takes ten years to get it.

Giancarlo was becoming my friend as well as my lover. But of course it was more than that. Sometimes he'd look at me – really look into my eyes – and I'd look back and feel a warm glow.

One day he arrived with a small carrier bag and said: 'I thought you would like this.' Inside was a delicately wrapped packet, all tissue paper and coloured bows, and inside this was a beautiful silk scarf with the purples and greys of the Monti Pisani, the mountains that lie behind Pisa.

My colleagues said: 'You look great.'

I felt great . . . and blissfully happy.

At the end of October Sarah came to visit. She had time on her hands because her teaching hours had been reduced. We had discussed our different situations in the past: me on an English contract and she – because she was Australian and couldn't get either an English or Italian contract, working freelance. There were advantages to her situation – like a better hourly rate and more freedom to decide which groups to teach. However, it was difficult for her financially during quiet periods.

It was a mild day and the autumn colours – the russets and yellows and burnt orange – were beginning to take hold of the countryside. We decided to walk the four kilometres round the walls of Lucca. As we strolled along, the fallen leaves crunching under our feet, Sarah asked me how it was going with Giancarlo.

'You were right,' I said. 'Nothing's too much trouble. He takes me out, thinks of nice things to do, buys me presents and makes me laugh. And he's very . . .' I hesitated, searching for the right word.

'Passionate?'

'Yes,' I confirmed. 'And romantic, and . . . involved.' I was having difficulty conveying a sense of this new experience: a man who was both sensual and mature.

'Enjoy it,' she said, 'and don't forget – Italian women always play hard to get.'

'I think it's too late for that. But there is one thing. At the weekends when he's tied up with his family, there's never any mention of introducing me, and he goes to dinner with friends without me.'

'Oh, that's normal in Italy. He can't introduce you to anyone – especially the family – unless he's really serious. It's a sign that he's going to marry you. You'll have to give it time.'

'It sounds like the 1800s.'

'More or less,' she said.

Although I'd had misgivings about sharing with so many younger women, it turned out to be surprisingly easy. The flat was peaceful during the day with everyone either at lectures or studying in their rooms. I taught mostly in the evenings, so I had lots of quiet time to myself. At the weekends, four of the girls went home, and the others went shopping, to the cinema or out with their friends. Perhaps it was because Italians are used to living in close family groups that there were none of the clashes or petty squabbles I'd heard about from my flat-sharing colleagues back in Sydney.

One day, over a breakfast cup of tea, Michela asked me: 'Is the food so very different in Australia?'

I'd fallen into the Italian habit of eating pasta every day, so they had no idea what the typical Australian 'cuisine' was. I started to describe what seemed to me the main differences, particularly that Australian food reflected its multicultural society and so we had dishes from all over the world.

'Why don't we cook a dinner together?' she asked. 'I'd love to try something new.'

Michela was a little unusual in this. Most Italians are firmly wedded to their pizzas, pastas and food that their mother – and grandmother – made. To my knowledge, there are just two restaurants in Pisa that serve foreign food. When I'd asked around my students at the school to get an opinion on how good they were, I drew a complete blank. No one had ever eaten there.

Thursday was the appointed evening. All the girls were in agreement, and offered to provide the wine and do the washing up. I decided on a Thai chicken dish, with ginger, spring onions and a hint of chili, served with rice. Michela helped with the preparations, chopping and slicing very efficiently. The others kept popping into the kitchen to check on progress. They were particularly intrigued by the way I cooked the rice Asian-style. In Italy, they told me, rice is eaten as risotto, cooked slowly, with water or stock added gradually until it ends up like a thick, mushy soup.

When we were ready, Katia lit the candles and Ilaria

opened the wine. This was going to be a proper dinner party. Antonella was the last to arrive. Being from a remote region of Sardinia, she looked at the food suspiciously.

'It's okay, Antonella,' I said, 'it's completely fresh, there are no . . .' I was searching for the word 'additives'. I didn't know it, so I guessed: 'No *preservativi* in the food.'

Silence. Complete silence. They all just looked at me. And then Michela started to laugh. She was the only one who knew for sure that there were, in fact, no condoms in the food.

In November it started to rain and turn cold. Central heating was included in our rent, but the box with the controls was locked. Michela told me that Signora Bucheri had the key, but if past years were anything to go by, she wouldn't be in a hurry to switch it on. She gave me the benefit of her four years experience living under the roof of the signora: 'She's a witch. A Sicilian witch, pure and simple. She's two-faced. She's nice to all the parents, but couldn't care less about the students.' From what I'd observed, it seemed a reasonable assessment.

Michela continued: 'Her husband died a couple of years ago, and when she mentions him now, she's in tears – crocodile tears. You should've heard the rows. She used to scream at him, throw things – you've no idea. And then her son took up with one of the students – a German girl who was staying in the room Antonella has now.' She rolled her eyes heavenwards. 'It was the end of the world. She wanted to throw her out, him out . . . In the end she came round, but it was pretty unpleasant for all of us for a while.'

I made an executive decision. I would buy a small electric fire, and hide it when the signora was on the prowl. I could slide it out of sight under the chest of drawers next to the plug. Perfect. Except for the day when the secretary called me to cover for a sick colleague. I unplugged the fire as usual, locked my door and cycled round to the school. The student didn't turn up and so after fifteen minutes I went home. When I opened the door to my room, there was an eerie orange glow coming from under the chest of drawers and the unmistakable smell of scorched wood. I'd unplugged the radio, not the fire. It took three days – and a can of air freshener – to get rid of the smell of charred wood. I tried not to think about the consequences had I not come home so quickly.

On the last Saturday in November, Giancarlo and I went to the truffle festival – *Sagra dei Tartufi* – in San Miniato, a small village clinging to the side of a hill near Florence. Truffles are found in very limited areas of Italy, and this was one of them.

'I didn't realise truffles grew outside France,' I commented as we drove through the countryside.

'These are a different species,' he told me. 'They're white, not black like the French ones, and cost a lot more because they're rarer.' I'd never even seen a truffle. They could be purple for all I knew. He continued: 'Truffles are so valuable, they use specially trained dogs to sniff them out. The dogs alone cost 20 million lire [$20 000] each.'

We stopped at a local *ristorante* and ordered pasta with truffles. The pasta arrived, followed by a special waiter with white gloves who grated bits of what looked like a dirty tennis ball over our plates. The perfume was strong and immediate: petrol. Truffles smell like petrol. The flavour, however, is delicate and strange, and unlike anything I'd ever eaten before. I decided that truffles were an acquired taste, and a ruinously expensive one at that.

As we were eating, I told Giancarlo about nearly setting fire to the house. He found it amusing, but then said: 'Seriously, are you cold at home?'

Well, yes, I had to admit that the flat wasn't very warm, and when I was working at my desk, I often wore a hat and scarf.

That evening there was a ring on the doorbell. Ilaria answered it: 'Susan,' she said, 'it's for you!'

'Come down!' said a male voice that I recognised immediately.

When I went down I found Giancarlo standing in the entrance hall with three carrier bags in his hands. In the first was a beautiful reddish-brown padded coat with a smart beige trim. In the second, a rollneck cashmere jumper in the same colour, and in the third was a pair of black leather gloves. 'I didn't know what to get you for Christmas,' he said, 'but I thought these could be useful.'

'But we're weeks away from Christmas!' I said, a little overcome.

He smiled: 'I always get important dates wrong.'

'Thank you,' I said. 'I've never had such beautiful presents. Would you like to come up?'

'No, no. I'm just off to a meeting, but I'll call you later.'

Four weeks later, Christmas really was upon us. My ticket to Ireland was booked and Giancarlo took me to the airport.

As we waited in the queue, he said: 'Let me know the time of your return flight and I'll collect you. And would it be all right to ring you at your daughter's?' I gave him the number, of course.

Ireland was under a foot of snow – crisp, white and beautiful. Hannah and I put on our wellingtons and crunched around, following the prints of the squirrels and leaving behind our own footprints, clear and defined. We built a snowman, squat with flat ears, and decided it looked like a koala bear.

Giancarlo rang the following day. Sam took the call: 'There's someone for you,' she said. 'He's foreign-sounding.'

We exchanged pleasantries, in Italian, and then Giancarlo said softly: 'I miss you.'

'I miss you too,' I replied.

When I hung up Sam looked at me with a half-grin, half-smirk: 'So, who was that?'

'A friend.'

'What sort of friend?'

'Mind your own business.'

'Oh, *that* sort of friend.'

I found myself thinking about Giancarlo often – replaying our lovely times together, and missing his touch. I wanted to buy him something for his *onomastico* (saint's day), which in Italy is celebrated more than birthdays. Giancarlo's *onomastico* was in January. I had no clear idea what to get until I saw a huge, elegant stainless steel bread bin. This was it. Not only was it a lovely shape but it was the perfect size for the large, oddly shaped bread that he ate with every meal.

Sam took one look at it and said: 'And how do you think you're going to get that back to Italy?' She had a point.

In the end, I carried it with me on the plane as hand luggage. The man at security looked at it suspiciously. This was Northern Ireland, after all. They were used to large, heavy metallic objects – but not for putting bread in. 'What's this?' he asked me. I told him.

'Don't they have bread bins in Italy?' he sounded sceptical. 'No, they don't.'

I don't think he believed me, but he let me take it through.

Giancarlo was at the airport to meet me. I saw his smile as I came through the arrivals hall, and felt relief and happiness. I was pleased to be back.

He took my luggage. 'What's this?' he said, indicating the bread bin.

'It's for you,' I said, 'for your *onomastico*.'

'For me? From Ireland?' It was a success. He was pleased: 'People only ever give me socks and whisky,' he said lifting the lid to inspect inside. 'It's lovely to have something personal.'

The barrier of the airport carpark was in total confusion. The cars were banked up, with drivers tooting and shouting the usual colourful *imprecazioni* (abuse). 'What's going on?' I asked.

'Oh,' he said with a resigned smile, 'the whole of Italy has been like this since New Year's day.'

'But why?'

'The introduction of the euro.'

Of course. I'd forgotten. He described a situation both funny and predictable: the banks hadn't printed enough banknotes, so the cash machines had run out. This had infuriated the shopkeepers, who relied on the post-Christmas sales to make their money for the year. It was illegal to accept the old lire – but as the banks didn't have any euro, that's all people had available. There were fights in shops, fights in the bank queues and an inevitable round of accusations apportioning blame, hours of television coverage, and suspicions that someone was getting very rich from the situation – probably the politicians – and that it was all one huge fraud. There's even a word in Italian for this type of institutionalised chaos: *un' italianata*.

We drove straight to his apartment. In the entrance hall of the building were, as usual, his bike and those of his neighbours. Chained up to his was another one, shiny green with gleaming metal work and a new saddle. It was – no, it couldn't be – *il cavallo verde*? 'How . . . what?' I spluttered.

He'd 'stolen' it from outside Signora Bucheri's house – used bolt cutters to break the chain – and then had it renovated.

'Thank you,' I said, 'that's the nicest thing anyone has ever done for me.'

He put his arms round me and said: 'I'd like to do lots of beautiful things for you.'

CHAPTER 11

A new year and a new resolution

Term began. This was the dark term. The festivities of Christmas and New Year were over and there were two months of cold, biting weather to face before the explosion of waxy-pink magnolias signalled spring. I sat in my room, warm and cosy now that the signora had finally, grudgingly, turned on the central heating. From my desk I could see the customers entering and leaving the bakery opposite. The warm smells of baking yeast and spices were a morning pleasure, and ensured I was always starving by lunchtime.

Giancarlo and I had been seeing each other for six months. In Cambridge all those years ago, when I'd declared I wanted to immerse myself in a foreign culture, falling in love hadn't been part of the plan. But perhaps it wasn't possible to experience the true Italy without love? It was, after all, the country of lovers and romance. But now what? Where was this heading? The answer came to me: I had to be patient. Things would become clear in time.

One day as I was planning lessons at my desk, there was a knock on the door. It was the signora. She explained that it was the custom in Italy for the priest to visit every house in his parish during Lent. She asked me to join the rest of the household in the kitchen.

There, in his black priestly robes, stood a short, stocky man with what appeared to be strands of tobacco growing out of his nose. He smelled like a goat. He looked at me with surprise, clearly surmising that I wasn't one of his flock, and broke into prayer. I joined in – where I could – watching the girls crossing themselves and doing the same. The priest then put his fingers in the holy water and – flick, flick – started splashing it around the kitchen. One particularly large drop hit me full in the face. As it slid down my cheek and came to a stop just above my chin, I realised that I was, indeed, truly blessed.

Apart from being the coldest term, the Easter term is also the busiest. I was given three new evening groups to teach, and had lots of requests to do private lessons at home. Giancarlo was also being stretched. As well as his teaching and departmental responsibilities in Pisa, he had to attend committee meetings in Rome. I never properly understood what these were, although he tried to explain them to me. It all sounded terribly complicated, and I concluded they were yet again part of the inevitable round of impenetrable Italian bureaucracy.

'Come with me,' he said. 'Let me show you Rome.' I thought

of Paul and our four days there two years earlier. Was Rome a place that worked its magic on every visit, I wondered, or only the first? I wasn't to find out that time. Giancarlo called me the day before our intended trip: 'I'm sorry,' he said, 'they've moved the dates. I have to be in Rome this evening. We'll go together another time.' I was disappointed, but understood. Work is work, after all.

Easter was early in 2002. I'd been working very hard and was pleased at the prospect of a break. I was also looking forward to seeing the family in Ireland, although I knew I would miss Giancarlo. Perhaps, I thought, next holiday he could come to Ireland too. I wanted him to meet my family, and we could visit Dublin and see something of Ireland together.

The scrap with the huge eyes was now a moving ball of energy: 'Ellie's a wriggly worm, Granny,' said Hannah, referring to her sister. '*And* she takes my toys.'

'Never mind,' I said. 'Let's go for a walk.' We put on our raincoats and wellingtons and splashed through the puddles and mud.

Giancarlo rang every day. 'So . . .' said Sam. There it was again, that quizzical tone.

'So what?' I asked.

'Is it serious? Don't tell me you're going to stay in Italy permanently.'

'Look,' I said. 'I don't know. It's early days. I haven't even met his family.'

'And if he asked you?'

'I don't know. Honestly, I really don't know.'

'Sorry,' she said. 'I think all this waiting around to hear from Australia is getting to me.'

'I'm sure it is,' I soothed. 'There's a lot of uncertainty. But it's only a question of time.'

We made Easter cards with yellow sticky paper and bits of cotton wool, and then hid Easter eggs around the house for the children to find. Meanwhile it rained and rained. When they took me to the airport, Hannah pressed her nose against the car window, and then blew me a kiss.

Giancarlo was at the airport to meet me, as I knew he would be. He hugged and kissed me. I was so happy to be back. We gabbled our news, trying to say everything at once and talking over each other.

He'd made supper at home. As I walked through the huge wooden front door of his apartment, he said: 'I thought it was time to do some decorating.'

I walked from room to room marvelling at the effect of the soft yellow paint that now covered the grey-green walls. It made the flat not only lighter, but also airier. I sat on the cream-coloured, heavy-cotton sofa in the sitting room, and looked around. The books and photos that had stood on the grey floor-to-ceiling bookcase were now displayed against gleaming jasmine-white paint. The dark antique table in the corner and the matching side tables had been polished to a deep shine. I had, I thought, never seen such a transformation.

Giancarlo took my hand and led me from the sitting room, down the corridor, past the spare bedroom and into the main bedroom, which, like the kitchen, looked out towards the mountains. It had been painted a deeper yellow – warm and not too bright. Exactly the colour of my flat in Sydney. 'It's lovely,' I said. 'It's my favourite colour.'

'I thought you'd like it. I imagine you miss the brightness of Australia. Perhaps this will help.'

Pisa was as cheerful as the newly painted flat, with the trees in full bloom and the dense smell of blossom in the air. We were moving into May, full of promise for the summer to come – and the end of term.

I rang Sarah: 'Fancy an evening out?'

'Too right,' she said. 'I've had a hell of a time. My brother came to stay with his girlfriend and they were fighting all the time and I kept getting caught in the middle. Families – what a nightmare! Thank God I live in Italy.'

We arranged to meet the following day. In the meantime, Tom called a meeting of all the teachers. He had some important business to discuss. We all assembled at the appointed hour, curious to hear what it was.

'Things aren't going well,' he said.

'Economic factors are pressing against us – the euro, the competition. We're all going to have to pull in our belts. If any of you have any ideas on how we can save money, I'd like to hear them.'

Just for a second my mind raced back to the photocopier incident of many months ago, and I wished that Poofta Bastard, with his arched eyebrows, exaggerated hairstyles and irreverent attitude, was still part of the team. I could imagine his response, his broad Australian accent and slow grin: 'Stop spending all the money on your ditzy wife, ya silly fucker!' However, we weren't to have the benefit of his input, and so were obliged at least to pretend to take it seriously.

Various suggestions were made, each one more ludicrous than the next. I kept quiet. I'd learned by now that the school – although a great place to teach – was a shambles from a management point of view, and that nothing suggested would ever get implemented. Tom would just have to dig deeper into his pockets. We were, after all, teachers not business managers, and I didn't imagine he'd have the nerve to suggest pay cuts given that the cleaning lady's hourly rate was more than ours.

Sarah and I met in our local trattoria at the corner of Via Arancia and Via Santa Maria that evening. She sailed in, black pants suit and top, black and white chequered scarf twirled around her neck, and the by now familiar blue earrings that perfectly matched her eyes. How does she do it? I thought. She always looks fabulous.

We had a couple of glasses of wine and started to discuss the staff meeting. One suggestion had been to increase class sizes – a self-defeating strategy because the quality of attention goes down, and the students feel they're not getting value for money.

Sarah was a good mimic. She managed to convey, with pregnant pauses and a suitably clipped, upper-class voice, the impression Tom gave of being on the point of saying something important, but then forgetting what it was. Soon we were both laughing uncontrollably: 'Hmm . . . Emilio, you could just sit on Giorgio's lap, and Chiara, there's room for you under the desk . . .'

It was the end of the evening. We'd had our *cantuccini* and *vin santo* and were both thinking about going home when Sarah suddenly said: 'Do you know the easiest way to get yourself killed in Italy? Cross the road on a zebra crossing. Believe me, they won't stop for you.'

Sarah, in a moment of haste, had forgotten this important fact. 'Yesterday I was late, and thinking about the lesson. I'd started to cross when I heard the squeal of brakes and a car – a blue car with two people in it – stopped just short of me.' She hesitated before saying: 'It was Giancarlo – with a woman.'

'What?' I said. 'Are you sure?'

'I was looking straight at him,' she said reluctantly.

'Did he see you? Did he recognise you?'

'I don't know . . . I think so.'

'And the woman?'

'Look, I wasn't going to tell you, but it didn't seem fair not to. It's probably nothing – a sister or a colleague.'

'Yesterday, you said. What time?'

'Just before four.'

'But Giancarlo had a meeting in Livorno yesterday,' I said. 'He didn't get back till just before dinner.' Something in my head went click. No, more like CLICK!

Sarah saw my face. 'Look,' she said, 'don't overreact. It's probably nothing. Think of all the lovely things he's done for you. Why would he bother if he's got someone else?'

I knew hers was the voice of reason, but I also knew – with

the same instinct that my mother had shown about my father – that this wasn't 'nothing'.

I tried to stay calm and put it out of my mind. After all, Sarah may have been mistaken, or perhaps Giancarlo had just forgotten to mention a change of plans.

The following evening at dinner I said: 'You know, you nearly ran Sarah over.'

'Who? Oh yes . . . Sarah. But when? Where?'

'On Monday, outside Centro Forum. She was on the zebra crossing.'

His eyes gave an involuntary flicker. 'Ah, yes.'

'You were with someone.'

'No, I don't think so. Monday, you say? I told you, I was in Livorno –'

'Enough,' I said, really quietly, almost in a whisper. 'Absolutely enough. You were with a woman.'

'Ah . . .' His face told me everything I needed to know.

'Listen,' I said, 'you can either tell me what's going on, or I'm leaving – now, this minute.'

'All right,' he said. He looked down and slightly away from me, his hands resting on the table. I knew this wasn't going to be pleasant. 'I wanted to tell you – was going to tell you – but then I . . . There is someone. Has been someone.'

'What do you mean – is, has been?'

'I've had a *rapporto* with someone. A few weeks ago I told her about you. She went mad – really berserk.' He looked up.

I stared at him, saying nothing.

'She was threatening everything – including harming herself. I didn't know what to do. I hadn't foreseen the possibility.' He paused briefly. 'You have no idea what Italian women can be like.'

Yes I had. Prima donnas, driven to madness by lying, deceiving men. I looked at him. His mouth was still moving, and I could hear the words, but somewhere else – my brain, my stomach – had gone into meltdown.

'How long has it been going on?' My voice sounded strange. I don't even know why I asked the question. What did it matter?

'Since my wife died.'

'And while we've been together?' But I already knew the answer.

'Yes.'

I wanted to scream. 'I'm leaving,' I said. 'I don't want to hear any more.'

'Please, it's not what you think . . . let's talk about it calmly. I should have told you . . . I wanted to tell you . . .'

I didn't hear the rest. I fled back along the corridor, through the entrance hall and down the stairs, two at a time, onto my bike and away.

The next morning, I cancelled my lessons and switched off the phone. I stayed in my room and raged and cried. How dare he? How could he? All schmoozy lovey-dovey and all the while he's got someone else. The bastard! The lying cheating bastard! Bloody men – bloody Italian men! And then I howled again. Why hadn't I spotted it sooner? Of course an attractive man – an Italian – would have some 'arrangement'. Why hadn't I asked him? Why had I been so sure he was 'the one'? How could I have been so stupid!

In the meantime, Giancarlo sent me a letter, handwritten and in impeccable English. He asked my forgiveness. It was truly over with the other woman, but it was difficult. In a small place, in a small circle . . .

I rang Sarah. 'Oh my God,' she said, 'I'm so, so sorry. Aren't they all complete bastards! Get away for a while – take a break. You'll see things better from a distance.'

I sent a short note to Giancarlo. I was going away. I'd contact him when I got back. I rang the school and told them there was an emergency and I had to leave for England immediately.

I went to Cambridge and stayed with Hans, who had visited me in Pisa, and his wife, Jean. I sat in their peaceful garden that Jean had so lovingly designed – apple trees and raspberries at the back, lawns and overflowing flowerbeds in the front – and tried to make sense of things. What should I do? Was it worth staying in Pisa now? Perhaps I should just go back to Sydney? Nothing spoke to me loudly and clearly. It was all confusion.

Hans said: 'Look, be fair. He handled it badly, but it's a very human dilemma. He didn't know he was going to meet you. And what was he supposed to do about her? Italy's feudal. Everything takes a long time.'

Jean nodded in encouragement. 'Of course,' she said, 'he should have told you. But, then again, you didn't ask. Perhaps he needed to be sure before he made a move.'

Were they right? I didn't know. But after a couple of days I calmed down and decided that when I got back, I would ring him and at least we could talk it through.

Hans and Jean drove me the forty minutes from Cambridge to Stansted Airport. As the car hummed down the motorway and through the pancake-flat East Anglian countryside, I thought about Giancarlo's confession. How did I know it was over with the other woman? He'd managed to cover it so well, and hadn't owned up until he was cornered. No wonder I hadn't met his family and friends. Under the circumstances, he was hardly going to invite me to a cosy Sunday lunch or a dinner party with his friends. And what about that meeting in Rome? Had they really changed the day? Could I now trust anything he said? I didn't know what I wanted anymore, except to stop feeling angry, disappointed and hurt.

At the airport check-in queue I spotted one of my colleagues from Pisa. She'd been nicknamed 'Gasbag', and after five minutes of her company it was obvious why. I didn't feel up to a verbal onslaught so I slunk behind the large man in front of me, trying to avoid her.

I'd settled on the plane, seatbelt fastened, book opened, when I heard a little yelp of glee: 'Oh, Sue – hi – you don't mind if I sit next to you, do you? It's nice to have someone to chat to!'

There was to be no quiet reading or gazing at the snowy Alps for me this time. Gasbag talked and shoved crisps in her mouth for the entire two-hour flight, stopping only to buy a Coca-Cola from the trolley. I don't know where I found the willpower not to throttle her. At the airport, I managed to give her the slip, settled on the No. 3 bus and watched with relief as the bus doors closed for the ten-minute trip into town.

Back in my room, I dialled Giancarlo's number. An answer machine kicked in. I didn't recognise the voice. It must have been the wrong number, I thought. Giancarlo didn't have an answer machine.

I dialled again. The same answer machine. 'I don't believe it!' I said. 'It's Susan. I'm back.'

He rang me that evening. 'I got the machine so I wouldn't miss your call,' he said. 'Let's have dinner. Let's talk.'

He looked terrible – pale and nervy. This wasn't like him. 'I'm sorry,' he said. 'I made a terrible mistake. I thought I could manage everything – that you wouldn't have to know. I was feeling dirty – terrible – I wasn't sure what to do.'

'But that's not fair,' I said. 'If you'd told me at the beginning, I wouldn't have got involved.'

'I know. That's why I didn't tell you.'

'But that's even worse. You were playing with me. I thought I loved you, but now I find you're someone different. How can I trust you?'

'That's serious,' he said. 'But please, give me a chance. Let's take it slowly . . . there's no hurry.'

I said, 'I'm not sure. Let me think about it . . .'

And he said: 'Take all the time you need.'

CHAPTER 12

Moving forward

I was in a state of confusion. Somehow I'd wandered onto the wrong set. Instead of playing Sleeping Beauty to Giancarlo's Prince Charming, I found myself acting the part of the wronged woman in something out of Chekhov. I didn't know whether this change of role would prove fatal to my feelings for Giancarlo, or just wounding. Until I knew that, there was nothing I could do. So I did nothing and tried not to think about it too much. It would take time, and he understood that, so we agreed to keep in touch but without pressure or expectations.

In the meantime, I needed some space of my own and decided to look for a flat. It was the middle of May. The academic year didn't end until June, but some of the students would already have left. I asked around in the staffroom and Jennifer told me that Marta, one of her advanced students, was moving at the end of the month. I rang her straight away.

Marta confirmed that there was a small flat available and the landlady, who lived next door, had asked her to find another tenant. The deal was cheap rent in return for English lessons for the two children of the family. I rang the landlady and made an appointment to visit.

To get to the large, rambling house in Via di Nudo – which appealed to me as an address – I went along the Arno, past the church with the leaning tower and then down a narrow lane. Although only ten minutes from the centre of Pisa, it had a distinct country feel. The houses were surrounded by gardens, many with *orti* (vegetable patches and fruit trees), and in the background were the beautiful, purple-green Monti Pisani.

The landlady, friendly and smiling, introduced me to her husband, a teacher at the local high school, and the two children, a girl of nine and a boy of six. They stared at me and giggled when I spoke. The girl, Chiara, seemed tall for her age. She was skinny and had long legs and long, wavy fair hair. She didn't look at all Italian. Davide resembled his mother – dark, stocky and with a gaze that took everything in.

The flat was self-contained and ran the length of the house. I guessed it had been built as a granny flat, or perhaps to house servants. There were two rooms, a sitting room with diner and kitchenette, and a large bedroom with French windows looking onto the garden and the mountains beyond. The bathroom was small, but everything was *lindo* – sparkling clean. The rent was reasonable and all the bills were up to date. House bills are one of the main areas of fraud against foreigners in Italy. You have to check that the bills you get actually correspond to your meter, and when you move in, you must ensure that the meter is on zero. Otherwise you might find yourself paying for the previous tenant, or – as happened to Sarah when she first arrived in Italy – paying for the landlady.

I told the landlady, Gabriella, and her husband, Franco, that I could move in at the end of the month. We shook hands and the children giggled again.

I went to tell Signora Bucheri that I was leaving. She was annoyed: 'How can I get someone else now? It's nearly the end of the year.'

She was right, of course. Term ended in June, but as she hadn't asked me to sign a contract so she wouldn't have to pay tax on my rent, she was already well ahead. The girls in the flat organised a farewell drinks party – *prosecco* and *pizzette* (bite-sized pizzas), and presented me with a teapot to take to the new flat. And as is the custom in Italy, we exchanged kisses and mobile phone numbers, even though it was unlikely we'd be staying in contact.

I rang Giancarlo and told him that I was moving and he offered to help. 'Please,' he said, 'let me do this for you.' He arrived early in the morning, parked his car outside and helped me up and down the stairs with my things. At one point we ran into Antonella, who was one of his students. Her eyes nearly popped out of her head. Professors are considered gods in Italy, and here was one lugging my suitcases down two flights of stairs.

Giancarlo kept his word. He didn't pressure me, and as the shock and anger lessened, I began to thaw. One day I called in to see him on my way to work and he said, 'I've been thinking, there's something I'd like to give you.'

It was the keys to his flat. I felt the weight in my hand: the large, straight iron key that unlocked the heavy wooden front door of the building, and the lighter copper key that opened the door of his apartment. These were the keys to his house. And to his heart?

He read my thoughts: 'I want you in my life,' he said. 'Please, call in when you like. Make yourself at home. It doesn't matter if I'm here or not.'

I kissed him on the cheek, smiled and put the keys in my bag.

Sarah came to see my new flat. 'Wow!' she said. She was looking at the newly whitewashed walls dotted with attractive prints and photographs, and the easy chairs covered with beige throwovers and checked blue and white scatter cushions. 'You know,' she said, 'this place feels really "you".'

'Wait till you see out the back,' I said.

I took her through the bedroom and out into the garden. We put two directors' chairs in among the pots of herbs and geraniums I'd bought at the local market, opened a bottle of icy cold local *prosecco* and started to talk.

'You know,' she said, 'I feel really guilty. I wish I'd kept my mouth shut about Giancarlo and that other woman.'

'Sarah, please! It was going to come out, and it was never going to be nice. You did the only thing you could. Really.'

But she didn't look entirely convinced. 'Have you decided what to do?' she asked.

'No, not yet.'

In the meantime, I was enjoying the children next door. Chiara was not only older but sharper than her brother and led the way. Davide, like so many younger brothers of older sisters, coasted along in her wake. They played me little duets – she on the piano, he on the violin – out of tune and out of time. Sometimes we sang songs together in English or played Snap or Happy Families, although I never managed to win.

Gabriella worked for the Ferrovia (the state railway) and Franco, who finished teaching at one o'clock, looked after the children in the afternoon while Gabriella was at work. He sometimes came in for a chat, usually bringing some cherries or other fruit from the *orto*. He'd been to America a couple of times and liked to practise his English. I enjoyed being near them. Their simple good-heartedness helped keep me balanced.

One evening Gabriella called in with a bottle of Limoncello – the strong, sweet liqueur made from lemons – and soon after Franco arrived. Gabriella lowered her voice and said, 'Susan, I've been meaning to ask you. What exactly *did* Bill Clinton do?'

'Um,' I replied, 'what exactly do you mean, what did he *do*?' Surely I didn't have to spell it out for her?

'Well,' she continued, 'was he caught up with fraudsters or were foreign influences at play?'

Franco was nodding in encouragement. Clearly they were of the same opinion, only I didn't know what it was. 'Look,' I said, 'he may well have been, but there's never been any proof of that. He was indicted for lying under oath and of course it's totally unacceptable to have a president engage in tawdry sex with one of the secretaries.'

'*Scherziamo* [You must be joking]!' said Franco. 'They drummed a perfectly good president – an intelligent and charismatic man – out of office over some little . . . *puttana* [call girl]!' he spluttered.

'We wouldn't have a politican left if they applied that rule here!' And then added: 'Are you sure?'

It is simply one of the many cultural differences. Sexual indiscretions – at least on the part of powerful men – are considered not only normal but somehow laudable. It's as if a man isn't a real man unless he's got a girlfriend tucked away somewhere. In fact a few years ago, following the death of a noted Rome surgeon, there was a television interview with his presumed widow – a beautiful older woman, puffy round the eyes from weeping. She was clearly desolate. She also wasn't his wife; she was his lover.

The real wife, also watching the program, was bemused. 'But who is she?' she enquired of her adult son, who was watching the broadcast with her. He gently told her. 'Well!' she said, and then added: 'All right, he may have cheated on me, but he never bored me.'

I was beginning to see that in Italian terms, my reaction to Giancarlo's situation would be viewed as an overreaction. The problem was that I wasn't Italian.

It was the first week in June and a month since the bombshell when I rang Giancarlo and invited him to drop by on his way home. I had deliberately kept myself busy working and doing up the flat, but in my quiet moments I found myself thinking about him more and more and realised how much I missed him. We sat in the garden facing the mountains, sipping long Campari and sodas. He was very quiet.

After a few minutes, he leaned across and touched my arm. 'Look,' he said, 'please tell me – do you see a future for us? Any sort of future?'

Something in me gave way. 'Yes,' I said. 'I think so.'

I took his hand and led him through the French windows into the house and my bedroom. There, slowly and gently, we made love. He held and touched me as though I was made of delicate Venetian glass which could shatter into a thousand pieces. And so we re-established our *rapporto*. It couldn't be what it had been. We'd both been bruised and hurt, but the affection we'd lost in the storm and its wake gradually began to re-emerge.

I told Sarah. 'Yes,' she said, 'time does heal. Take it slowly. Don't rush anything. Try to keep it simple and enjoy things together.'

The other woman, however, wasn't going to give up so easily. Their lives had been entwined. She'd devoted years to him, and now she had nothing to lose. She phoned him, she contrived to meet him; she brought in friends to plead on her behalf. There were occasions when they met because they had friends in common; there were awkwardnesses and evasions. It was inevitable. They had the same circle of friends. I tried to be reasonable and put things in perspective. Largely

I succeeded. But sometimes I felt rage and jealousy even as I was trying to forgive and forget.

One day towards the middle of June, Giancarlo said: 'It's *Luminara* next week. Why don't we invite some people for drinks?'

Luminara is the evening set aside to celebrate the patron saint of Pisa. People in every *palazzo* up and down both sides of the river place candles around the windows, and hundreds of waterlily-shaped candles are floated on the river. We asked Lisa and Gianni from La Spezia, Sarah and her boyfriend, Fabrizio, and two of Giancarlo's work colleagues and their wives.

It was good to see Lisa again. We phoned each other occasionally, but it wasn't easy to find time to chat. She was looking radiant – now married and four months pregnant, slightly rounder and the picture of good health and happiness. She and Gianni were looking to buy a flat but were meeting the usual obstacles of unsuitable places, high prices, or exaggerated promises from builders. In the meantime, they were renting in Lerici, where Shelley had drowned in the bay. 'Come and see me,' she said. 'It's a simple journey – a train and then a bus to the door, just like the old days!' I promised I'd visit before the baby was born.

We drank *grappa* and *digestivi* (strong and bitter liquors) and ate *dolcini* (little cakes), and as the sun set over Ponte di Mezzo and the river, we gathered round the windows to watch the riverside buildings gradually fade into thousands and thousands of flickering lights. I realised that this was the first occasion on which Giancarlo and I had 'come out' as a couple. It was, however, in familiar surroundings and there had been Sarah and Lisa to chat to in English. I'd had a great time. The next social fixture, however, wasn't so easy.

The following evening, Giancarlo and I were sitting at his kitchen table chatting when the phone rang. 'It's Pamela,' Giancarlo said, holding his hand over the receiver, 'she and Giorgio have invited us for dinner. Would you like to go?'

These were two of his closest friends; they'd known each other for years. Giancarlo really was making a serious effort to include me in his life. 'Yes,' I said, 'that would be nice.'

Pamela was American but had lived in Italy for a long time. Giorgio was an aristocrat, but as the monarchy had been abolished in Italy after the war – the people voting decisively against their king, who had fled to save his own skin – it didn't mean much. Unless, of course, you counted the mansion, the land, forests and properties, and fabulous art collection.

The evening arrived and as we drove up to the imposing façade of the mansion, complete with tower and chapel, I felt a stab of nerves. This wasn't my milieu, and I couldn't even speak Italian properly. Pamela, however, was charming and immediately put me at my ease. She said – from her own experience, I imagined – 'Just smile and listen.' Giorgio, thin and wiry with a mop of thick grey hair, didn't speak English, but made small talk in Italian and smiled and nodded encouragingly.

It was a dinner party for eight. The other guests – all Italians – were an architect and his lady friend, a historian, a teacher and her scientist husband. Drinks were served in a reception room with family portraits and tasteful furniture. The historian, a woman in her fifties with a kind face and a remarkable resemblance to Princess Margaret, said: 'I have an Irish friend who's been here for twenty years. She's learned the language, but says she'll never adjust to the culture.' And then she laughed.

Why was she laughing? She seemed amused at some secret that she had no intention of sharing with me.

Dinner was served in the dining room, which was also tastefully furnished with antiques and *objets d'art* that must surely have been family heirlooms. I was placed between the scientist and the architect, neither of whom addressed a word to me. How rude, I thought, remembering my English up-bringing, which was all about manners and putting people at their ease. And then I realised: Pisa is essentially feudal. The host and hostess were the lord and lady of the manor, and I – as the blow-in on Giancarlo's arm – came last. I wasn't blue-blooded, didn't have a prestigious occupation and couldn't even speak their language.

Finally and thankfully we adjourned to another stylish room, this time with an open fire and large comfortable sofas. The walls were covered with antique prints of water-birds. For the sake of something to say, I commented: 'Oh, how lovely. I love birds!'

Princess Margaret burst out laughing again, and then fell silent. What was it this time? What the hell was she laughing at? Rude cow! I was fuming.

We left at one in the morning. This, for Italians, is considered the normal hour to go home, if not perhaps a bit on the early side. Evening events like film screenings and theatre performances begin between 9 pm and 10 pm to allow time for dinner at 8 pm, and reflect the fact that everyone has had a three-hour break during the day. I had found the dinner both interesting and disturbing. It wasn't every evening I found myself dining with the upper echelons of European society, but on the other hand I'd felt uncomfortable. The world of these people was very different from mine, and Pamela had been the only one who made any effort to put me at my ease. I still didn't know why Princess Margaret had laughed at me. I asked Giancarlo.

'Well,' he said, 'you said you liked birds.'

'Yes, it's true. I do like birds. What's so funny about that?'

'In Italian 'birds' has a double meaning – it can also mean male genitals.'

Oh great! I'd openly declared my liking for male 'bits' to the crème de la crème of Pisan society. 'Well,' I said defensively, 'I think it's rude to laugh at the innocent mistakes of others – and I think it's rude to make no effort to converse with strangers.'

He could feel the heat in my comments: 'Don't take it seriously,' he said. 'It was just a stupid dinner party. They aren't used to meeting people from outside their own little group. Pamela was nice to you, wasn't she?'

'Yes,' I conceded, 'she was lovely.'

'Before she met Giorgio, her life was not unlike yours.'

'In what respect?' I was curious. There weren't too many obvious parallels.

'Well, she'd lived and worked in several countries. She was here on holiday from Africa when she met Giorgio.'

It was true. Over time Pamela and I found many things in common, and became friends.

The road home passed through narrow village streets, and then opened out onto the Pisan plains under the mountains. We drove along a straight stretch of road and then slowed almost to a halt to take a sharp left-hand turn. As we negotiated the corner, an imposing figure appeared from the shadows and thrust the biggest pair of bare breasts I'd ever seen against the windscreen of the car. I gave a yelp of surprise – well, shock, really – but Giancarlo kept driving with perfect equilibrium. 'I see you haven't met the ladies of the night before,' he said.

Well, yes, I've taken the occasional stroll around Kings Cross after hours, but I'd never seen anything like this. There were at least eighty 'ladies of the night' spread out along this stretch of isolated country road, each one more provocative than the other. The night air was decidedly chilly, but all of them were scantily clad and showing great swathes of leg, backside and chest. Their gestures were a mixture of leering and seductive. 'Good grief!' I exclaimed. 'Is this usual?'

'Oh yes, perfectly,' Giancarlo replied. 'Every now and again the police round them up. But probably money passes hands, because they're soon back in business.'

According to an article I read later in the local paper, they were all Brazilian transvestites. Some have had operations to make them female, others not. They can earn up to 1000 euro a night ($2000), and most of their customers are homosexual. However, they also have straight clients who, apparently, are not committing adultery by having sex with men dressed as women, which is a bizarre little twist on religious morality.

Two days later Giancarlo and I were sitting in a shady spot in my garden drinking ice-cold beer. It was the end of June, and the weather had turned hot. My little apartment, which had been pleasant a month ago, was close and airless. Fortunately, there was the garden to escape to.

'There's a family lunch on Sunday,' Giancarlo said. 'Would you like to come?'

The Italian family is the basic economic and social group. They do have friends and acquaintances – lots of them – but friends aren't ever in the same league as family. As a family member, you have obligations – Sunday lunches, meals and celebrations, visits if someone is ill, and generally pulling together. If you are in difficulty, however, you will be looked after by the family in turn. Family members ring each other nearly every day – two-minute phone calls just to catch up – and everyone knows what everyone else is doing. It's not unusual for an Italian family to occupy different apartments in the same house, all keeping an eye on one another but living independently at the same time. They don't think about it because for them it's how it's always been. To Anglos, it takes time to get used to and can feel claustrophobic.

This was the real test – not only of Giancarlo's feelings and intentions towards me, but of mine towards him. Had I forgiven him? Was I willing to be acknowledged by his family as 'the one'? Did I really want to take this next step? 'Yes,' I said simply.

Lunch was at his sister's house. One of Giancarlo's sons would be there with his family, as would the other sister with her family. I counted ten people in all.

Sunday came around and by then I did feel nervous.

'There's nothing to be anxious about,' Giancarlo reassured me. 'My family is very informal and they'll make you feel welcome.' He gave me a hug and a kiss and said: '*Andiamo* [Let's go]!'

He was right. The two sisters, Anna Maria and Rosa, were warm and natural: with surprisingly blue eyes, they resembled each other but not him. Anna Maria was married and her husband, Aldo, spoke reasonable English. Rosa had never married, but had worked in industry and had been a trade union leader. I noticed she had books on trade union law and feminism on the bookshelf.

Lorenzo, who was taller than his father, smiled and chatted to me in English. He and his wife, Patrizia, had travelled extensively, and had spent a few months in Perth. She was nearly as tall as me, blonde and very attractive. This was so different from the stuffy dinner party. I was completely at ease. They talked about everyday things – life, politics, events – in an open way and, as is the Italian custom, all together. They included me but didn't bombard me, and made it clear that I was most welcome.

We ate a typical Sunday lunch – pasta, chicken with a long

stringy green vegetable which looked like dark celery (I later found out it was thistle), followed by little cakes and coffee. The wine flowed and everyone, including the three-year-old grandson who was clearly used to these lunches, seemed to be enjoying themselves.

Then, just as the *grappa* and coffees were being served, a huge crack sounded, like a whiplash, and the central foot of the dining room table, unable to bear the weight of any more bottles or plates, sheared in half. With it went one half of the table, depositing the remains of the lunch into our laps. It was a spectacular moment – a genuine *italianata*. Rosa was mortified, everyone was scrabbling around trying to hold things, retrieve things and get bits of food out of their clothing. The noise and confusion were deafening – through the roof – and all the while the three-year-old gazed on as if nothing had happened.

The next day I rang to thank Rosa for her hospitality, and she said that they hoped to see me again very soon. The lunch – despite the table – had been a success.

CHAPTER 13

How the story ends ...

It was the beginning of July. The summer term was at an end and I – as had become my habit – planned to go to Ireland for August, leaving July free. As the weather got hotter and hotter, I realised that my little flat – so cool and pleasant only a month earlier – was now uninhabitable. The metre-thick stone walls in such a small space acted like storage heaters, radiating a thick hellish heat into the rooms. The humidity was appalling. I gulped water at the same rate as air, splashing my face and arms in a useless attempt to keep cool. My wilting body stuck to my dress, which in turn stuck to the chair. This, I thought, is straight out of Dante's Inferno.

I tried opening the double doors front and back in order to create a through breeze. This gave me a little relief, but only when there was some movement in the stagnant air. The open doors did, however, let in industrial quantities of frenetic black flies during the day, and buzz-bomb mosquitoes at night. I was, I decided, fighting a losing battle against the forces of nature.

I spoke to Franco and Gabriella: could we look at getting flyscreens for the doors? No, they said. They were sorry, but there was nowhere to fix them that didn't impede access and wasn't illegal. The best they could offer were heavy net curtains front and back. These, I realised, would stop what little airflow there was, but not the mosquitoes. They would also block out my view of the mountains.

'We don't usually have this problem,' Gabriella told me, 'because our tenants go home for the holidays.' She continued: 'They are also out during the day in the winter, so I hope you don't suffer from the cold because in winter the heating only comes on in the evenings.'

Of course, the flat was usually let to students. Great! My choice was to suffer in silence, or buy fans and heaters and rack up extortionate power bills. I thought back to the bills Lisa and I had received two years before and shuddered.

Giancarlo came to my rescue: 'To hell with it, why don't we go to Sardinia for July? I finish on the seventh, which would give us three weeks. We can take the car, drive around a bit, stay in little hotels and relax. The sea in Sardinia is exceptional and there's always a cool breeze.'

So, to my great relief, two days later we were in the car on the way to catch the night ferry from Livorno to Olbia, the main port on the northeast coast of Sardinia. As we dutifully waited in line, I noticed the ship had a big blue spouting whale painted on its side: Moby Line, it proudly proclaimed. 'Who thinks up these things?' I asked Giancarlo. I wasn't entirely happy about spending the night in the guts of a whale, even a metaphorical one.

The interior of the boat was as I imagined a cruise ship to be: themed sections for the different social groups. There was an elegant restaurant with thick carpets, soft lights and music, and waiters gliding around in short white jackets and bow ties; an 'executive' area, with flat-screen computers on minimalist black desks hooked up to the latest telecommunications; and a 'pub' full of foreign tourists and tobacco smoke. 'It's like Disneyland, isn't it?' Giancarlo commented.

We chose a self-service restaurant with Italian food, and after a post-supper stroll round the upper deck taking in the clear night air and thankfully calm sea, we retired to our cabin.

Early the next morning we were woken by the blaring of the public address system: 'Good morning, ladies and gentlemen. We will be docking in Olbia in half an hour. Please start making your way to your cars.' Just for a second, I was back at boarding school on a freezing February morning, racing to the bathroom and to get dressed before Matron appeared. I hauled the covers back and shot out of bed before realising my mistake.

'What are you doing? Come here!' Giancarlo pulled me gently back into bed and leaned across and kissed me. Then: 'Let's go and have a look at Sardinia,' he said.

Before clambering down the four flights of metal steps into the fume-filled depths of the ferry, we went on deck for my first glimpse of this low-slung and surprisingly green island, with hills and mountains tapering off into the distance. 'What do you think?' Giancarlo asked me, putting his arm around my waist.

'It looks like a group of giant green hippopotamuses coming out of the water,' I replied.

He grinned at me as if to say, you're slightly mad, but I like it.

We drove from Olbia north along the coast to Porto Cervo. This is the most exclusive and expensive place on what is already an exclusive and expensive island. It's like a holiday compound for seriously rich people, and could have come straight out of *Dallas*. The purpose-built complex of designer shops (with not a price tag in sight) might as well have displayed a sign on its gilded arched entry saying 'Do not enter unless you are loaded'. Although I was, for me, looking quite smart in a pale lilac linen dress and sling-back sandals, I felt underdressed as the women swished past in little silk tops and beautifully cut pants. Everything about them – from their designer sunglasses to their little pointed shoes – screamed money, money, money.

We drove further round the bay. The sea – clear, still and sparkling blue – was, as Giancarlo promised me, exceptional. I couldn't wait to get away from the fashion show and have a dip. Along the road, Giancarlo pointed out where the Aga Khan had his compound, complete with helipad. And there was the holiday village of Silvio Berlusconi, Italy's controversial prime minister. One thing, however, not disputed is his wealth: he's the richest man in Italy. On we went, past the ranches and villas of football players, models and celebrities. I could, just for a second, hear the voice of my mother, a product of her own Victorian English upbringing, saying: 'Oh dear, how terribly . . . *vulgar.'*

We were now at the northern tip of Sardinia, but this glittering ghetto wasn't for us. Giancarlo consulted the map, drove a little further and then took a left turn towards the centre of the island and away from Babewatch Beach.

Sardinia is an island roughly 200 by 100 kilometres, and although it is part of Italy, the people – as was shown in the genome project – have a different genetic makeup. It's not known where they came from originally, but they tend to be short and dark, rather like the people from southern Italy. They have their own customs, habits, and a language which is nothing like Italian. They have also, almost certainly due to their isolation, spawned a culture of bandits. Over the centuries these bandits, who mainly operate in the isolated central areas of Sardinia, have refined their activities from sheep stealing to kidnapping rich foreign visitors for ransom. In fact, following an ugly kidnapping in the 1970s, one involving the cutting off of a young man's ear, many rich foreigners sold up and found safer holiday homes on the French Riviera.

We were heading for Orgosolo, an hour south, and right in the heart of bandit country. As we drove inland, the countryside became hilly and then mountainous, but all the while it remained a deep, lush green. Along the road were the biggest prickly pears I've ever seen. The Italians call them *fichidindia* – Indian figs. The road narrowed to little more than a lane, and went up and up until we could see the grey-tiled roofs of Orgosolo in the distance.

As well as being a bandit stronghold, Orgosolo has a proud communist tradition which is manifest in graffiti. Practically every house has on its walls a design – perfectly painted – of some incident from socialist history. We wandered from house to house, as if visiting a giant outdoor art gallery, Giancarlo explaining the paintings that weren't obvious, and translating the captions. Many of the characters were holding fierce-looking serrated knives. These, Giancarlo told me, were a type of knife made in Sardinia for centuries and used by the bandits in their nefarious activities. My favourite was a life-sized picture of Desmond Tutu in his bishop's robes, holding a Bible against the backdrop of Africa. He is saying: 'They came to our land bringing us Bibles. In exchange, they left us their Bibles and took our land.'

We stopped at the local bar. As we walked in, the heads of the men sitting at the round tables playing cards turned to look at me, and followed my every step towards the table in front of the picture window overlooking the valley. 'They don't try to hide their curiosity, do they?' I said as I sat down.

'No, not in these small, isolated places. Our visit will give them something to talk about for days, especially as you're clearly a foreigner.'

I'd never been openly stared at in this way before, and it made me feel uncomfortable. I preferred being on the side-lines, but of course I'd been taught to never, never openly stare myself.

'It's like they were *undressing* me!' I complained to Giancarlo later.

He grinned. 'Here we have another example of the cultural

divide. An Italian woman would have taken it as a compliment.'

'I don't regard being gawped at by a group of decrepit bandits with flick knives particularly complimentary!'

We decided to stay the night in the mountains before driving down to the coast the following day. We wanted to find a quiet seaside spot to spend the rest of our holiday. As we drove around the twisty mountain roads, I understood how it was possible for the bandits to hide out for years without being caught. The terrain was rough and craggy, with few tracks or roads, and virtually impenetrable.

That evening, we stayed in a small hotel at Oliena, another isolated mountain village a little further north. We sat with the locals – who were more polite than the lot in Orgosolo and didn't stare – in the only restaurant and ate *malloreddus'*, a Sardinian pasta shaped liked gnocchi with a sauce made from lamb and spices, and drank the local dry red, Canonau.

The next morning, which was predictably clear and sunny, we drove for two hours in the direction of the sun until we reached the sea, took the coast road south and cruised along waiting for inspiration. I liked this approach. We didn't plan too much, but responded to ideas as they came to us. If we saw an unusual building or a stunning view, we stopped to look. We took little walks, stopped for coffee or beer when we felt like it, and passed the day in pleasant, aimless wandering. I was interested to see the different aspects of Sardinia, but what I really wanted to do was relax. It had been a long couple of months, and now I wanted to simply unwind.

We both saw it at the same time – a small roadside sign that said 'Apartments to let'. We drove down a stone track until it opened out into a small complex set among pine trees. The single-storey whitewashed units, each with a small garden, faced the estuary of a narrow river that fed into the sea. I looked around. All I could see, apart from the units and pine trees, were sand and sea: a sea so luminously turquoise it hurt my eyes to look at it. Perfect! Giancarlo went to investigate. He came back smiling. It was decided. We'd spend the rest of our holiday here.

Life at the beach was one of complete relaxation, with the days soon forming themselves into a regular pattern. We got up late and had breakfast – coffee and panetone, the soft, yellow bread-cake – at the table under the umbrella, which also served as protection from the falling pinecones. These, once they left the trees, took on the speed and energy of a rocket and could break your head in two.

We then drove to the *panificio* (bread shop) in the nearby village to get the bread for the day, the *supermercarto* for provisions, and *fruttivendolo* for salad and fruit. Giancarlo explained the different cuts of meat in the butcher, and types of fish at the fishmonger. For me it was a bewildering array, but for him shopping for food was as much a passion as cooking it. We finished by having a cappuccino at the local bar before collecting the newspapers from the *giornalaio*.

Once home, it was time for a stroll along the seashore, picking up gleaming seashells and on one occasion finding a transparent, mushroom-shaped jellyfish with tentacles half a metre long. The sea was calm with gently lapping waves. It was a delight to swim rather than be pounded by surf while trying not to lose my bikini, like back in Sydney. We took strolls round the pine wood, meeting fellow visitors on the way.

As the days progressed, our walks became interspersed with polite chitchat and catching up with the daily news of the other people. As nothing ever happened, these conversations were not only predictable, but also easy to follow, thereby not putting too much pressure on my partially addled brain. Italians, being sociable, soon started issuing invitations, and within a week we were lunching or dining with other people every day.

Lunch – perhaps *triglia* (mullet), *spaghetti allo scoglio* (with seafood) or a local egg and cheese pie with glazed onions on the top, together with the obligatory wine and water – was followed by a short snooze. At six o'clock we'd shower and sit in the garden drinking chilled *prosecco* with one of our – by now – group of friends. I still found it tiring trying to follow the conversation as Italians tend to talk quickly and all at once. However, I noticed I was getting more proficient, and told myself it was just a matter of time before I'd be able to keep up.

I loved being at the unit sitting under the umbrella with the musty perfume of the pine trees, and gentle pace of life. No wonder Italians are one of the longest-lived races on earth, I thought. Why would you die when you can live like this? I believe I could have stayed at the seaside for months without getting bored or feeling the need to move on to something else. But inevitably, the finishing line appeared in sight. Only too soon it was time to start planning our departure: the cleaning, packing and two-hour drive to catch the ferry. I didn't want to leave. I had sunk into such a deep, hedonistic torpor – sun, swimming, afternoon naps, reading and gentle strolls – how would I adjust to the life of granny of two small children that awaited me in Ireland?

But we still had one more evening, and decided to go to a local seafood restaurant on the beach. The dinner was to be a celebration of the time we'd spent together: peaceful, relaxed and tender. As we sat at our outdoor table overlooking the sand, Giancarlo asked 'What's your opinion of Sardinia?'

'It's a very special place,' I replied. 'I can see why you love it.'

'Perhaps we can come back again next year. What do you think?'

I hesitated. I had been trying not to think too much about next year. My mind automatically started computing at the speed of light: would I be here next year? I was in love with Giancarlo; my flat was hopeless; I liked my job; I hardly earned enough to live on . . . The flow of neurons was stopped by the arrival of the waiter with two dishes: oysters for me, and a fish soup for Giancarlo. The oysters were smaller and stronger than Sydney oysters but with the same salty bite that I love. After a plate of Sardinian ravioli filled with fish and spinach, together with a bottle of chilled white, we took off our shoes and walked slowly back along the beach in the warm shallows.

Back at the unit, Giancarlo took my hand and led me to

the bedroom. He took my face in his hands and gently kissed my neck. I felt something well up – 'Urghh . . . oh . . . *scusami!*' I raced to the bathroom, hung over the toilet bowl and vomited and vomited. I thought it was never going to stop. I lurched back into the bedroom and collapsed on the bed. 'Oh God, I'm sorry!'

Giancarlo felt my brow. 'Why are you sorry? You're sick, you're burning up. Stay there, I'll be back in a second.'

I managed to pull off my dress and put on the white cotton tee-shirt I used for round the house. Giancarlo returned with towels and a bucket of water with ice cubes in it. He wet the towels, wrung them out and used them to wrap my shaky limbs.

'We must get your temperature down,' he said. He reached for his mobile, rang a number and spoke to someone quickly in Italian. It was one o'clock in the morning. I hoped this was someone he knew well.

'I just rang a friend,' he said. 'He's a doctor; we were at school together. He said to sip fluids, take paracetamol and if you keep vomiting, take you to hospital: you may need a drip to get fluids into you. I think it was the oysters,' he concluded with a wry smile.

I shivered and shook, too feverish to care that this was the last night of our holiday. Giancarlo lay beside me holding my hand. Every so often he mopped my brow and encouraged me to take sips of lightly sugared water. A few hours later the crisis had passed, but I still felt terrible: like an old hag – sticky hair, dry, cracked lips and shaking hands.

The next morning I wasn't sure if my legs would hold me

up, but with Giancarlo's help, I managed to get dressed. How bad is this, I thought. Here is the man of my dreams helping me to put my clothes on. I thought of the well-groomed, chic Italian women and considered my own sorry state. The comparison was truly odious: there was nothing the slightest bit chic about this situation. But Giancarlo seemed more focused on sorting things out than caring about how I looked.

'Don't worry,' he soothed. 'If you're not well enough to travel, we'll go to a hotel.'

I took a deep breath. 'We can't stay here because the unit's been re-let, so why don't we try for the boat?'

'Are you sure you feel up to it?'

I grimaced. 'If it gets too much, you can shove me out at the nearest rubbish tip.'

'Well, if you can joke, you can't be too sick.'

I hoped he was right.

He put the seat back in the car and made me comfortable with a pillow and light cover. I lay on what had become almost a full-size bed, truly grateful that Italian cars are designed to have sex in. In the meantime, Giancarlo packed the bags, cleaned the unit and returned the keys to the manager.

We drove slowly back to Olbia, me flat on my back sipping water through a straw, Giancarlo with his tanned elbow resting on the open window, looking like he was cruising home from a tennis championship. At the port he went to speak to someone in the shipping office. They arranged a wheelchair, together with a thickset man in a uniform to push it. At the cabin door, Giancarlo tipped the man and helped me through the door. The cabin was obviously first class. It was spacious, with carpet on the floor and twin beds with crisp cotton sheets. Just what I needed! I pulled off my dress, got in between the cool sheets and fell asleep.

When I woke up hours later, the room was in darkness and there was no sign of Giancarlo. I felt a moment's panic. Had he left me here? Hell, what was I going to do now? I turned on the bedside light. There was a message propped on the shelf next to my mobile phone: 'I'm in the restaurant. Call me.'

I decided to wait. He'd had a difficult day. At least he could have dinner in peace. I fiddled with the remote control, and the monster TV in the corner burst into life. A fellow in a mustard jacket who looked like Charlie Chaplin was directing some sort of phone-in program. On a long, narrow table, ten identical puffy cream buns were lined up, each one carefully marked with a number. Nine cream buns, Charlie told us, had cream in them, and one had anchovy. The viewers had to ring in and say which bun they thought contained the anchovy. The choice having been made, a pink, frilly 'babe' bit into the bun, smiled, opened her mouth and confirmed the contents to the studio audience. This was clearly a game of great skill. I watched, too weak to react, as three viewers in turn chose the wrong bun. What was the prize, I wondered – an evening out with Charlie?

The cabin door opened at this point and to my relief Giancarlo stood outlined in the doorway. 'Oh, good, you're awake. Why didn't you ring?'

'I thought you might like to have your dinner hot. In any

case, I've been properly entertained here.' I indicated the TV. Giancarlo turned to look just as Charlie, with a grotesquely salacious look on his face, bit into the tenth and final bun.

'It's amazing, isn't it?' said Giancarlo, shaking his head. 'We've become a nation of morons.'

We arrived back in Pisa early the following morning. I still had two days before I left for Ireland. 'Look,' Giancarlo said, 'you can't stay in your flat. You need to keep cool, and have someone keep an eye on you. Why don't you pack some things and come and stay in the spare room?'

I didn't argue. I knew he was right. My flat would be intolerably hot, there were no provisions and I wasn't up to doing anything.

We spent two quiet days together in the cool comfort of his flat by the river. He cooked while I read and listened to the radio. In the evening we walked along the river, he holding my arm in the Italian fashion as we watched the sun go down over Ponte di Mezzo.

The next day was my last day with Giancarlo. I was off to Ireland for four weeks and he was moving to the holiday house at Calambrone for August. Of course I wanted to see the family, but this time it was different. I didn't want to leave Giancarlo. The years of work, bringing up children and trying to find my way alone in the world had led me to this: a man who was patient enough to know me, accepting of what he found, and most of all wanted to be with me. I'd come to Italy in search of a foreign experience, and I'd found my other half. I pulled myself up. I didn't want to spoil my last day with thoughts about the past or concerns for the future. I looked at Giancarlo and felt an overwhelming tenderness.

'I've been thinking,' he said. 'You may not feel it's a good idea, but my house is big enough for us both . . .' His voice trailed off. He was obviously having difficulty saying what was on his mind. 'Look, I know I'm older than you . . . You could have your own study. I wouldn't interfere . . .

'Oh, what the hell! When you return from Ireland, come and live with me. What do you say?'

This time I didn't need to weigh things up. 'Yes,' I said. 'I say yes.'

Glossary

alimentari	grocers
amici del cuore	friends of the heart
anche a te	you, too
antipasto misto	mixed hors d'oeuvre
a tavola	at the table
ballo	dance
bambini	children, girls and boys
banconota	banknote
bello	beautiful
bocca	mouth
brutto	ugly
Buon Anno	Happy New Year
buona fortuna	good luck
buona notte	good night
buona sera	good evening
buongiorno	good day

cantina	wine cellar
carciofi	artichokes
carretto	cart
case chiuse	literally: closed houses (brothels)
cavallo	horse
cena	dinner
che sara', sara'	what will be, will be
ciao!	hi! hello! (also: 'bye! see you later!)
cipolle	onions
colazione	breakfast
conchiglia	shell
condito	seasoned, flavoured
coniglio	rabbit
copisteria	photocopy shop
cucina	cuisine, kitchen
elettricita'	electricity
facciamo cosi'	let's do it like this
fichidindia	prickly pear
fidanzata	girlfriend
fidanzato	boyfriend
forchetta	fork
fruttivendolo	greengrocer
gelateria	ice cream parlour
ghiozzo	rough (person)
giornalaio	newsagents

giubileo	jubilee
grazie	thank you
hotel modesto	cheap hotel
imprecazioni	swearwords
inclusa nel prezzo	included in the price
in punto	precisely
liscio	smooth
lupo	wolf
miracoli	miracles
mi scusi	excuse me (formal)
multa (multe)	fine (fines)
niente	no, nothing
nipoti	nephews, nieces, grandchildren
non si puo'	you can't
onomastico	saint's day
ora	the time, now
orto	vegetable garden
palazzo	building
parolacce	bad words
passaporto	passport
passeggiata	stroll or gentle walk
per favore	please
piazza	square, place

pinguino	penguin
pizzette	bite-sized pizzas
prepagato	prepaid
preservativi	condoms
principianti	beginners
puttana	callgirl
quale	what, which
rapporto	relationship
rompi palle	ball-breaker
sagra	festival
salotto	drawing room
salumeria	delicatessen
scheda telefonica	phone card
schifezza	a piece of rubbish, worthless
scusami	excuse me (formal)
signora	madam
sta' ferma!	sit still!
supermercato	supermarket
tipo	sort, type
tabaccaio	tobacconist
va bene	all right, okay
vaporetto	water bus
venga	come
venga pure	come along
verde	green

Questions for reading groups

1. How would you adjust to life in a new culture? What do you see as the major issues?
2. 'All you need is love.' Is this true?
3. What aspects of Italian life would you find appealing?
4. *Leaning Towards Pisa* is described as 'an Italian love story'. How would you describe it?
5. Which of the places described interests you most, and why?
6. Would you consider the Italian approach to food a celebration of life or a national obsession?
7. Music and art are integral to Italian life. What part do they play in your culture? What would you say are your culture's main shared interests?
8. 'Italian women are judged on how stylish and well-groomed they are.' What are the advantages and disadvantages of the Italian focus on '*La Bella Figura*'? Would you like to live with that emphasis in your life?

9. How does Italian society as described in *Leaning Towards Pisa* differ from your own?

10. 'You cannot live in Italy without being aware of the influence of the church'. What aspects of life is the author referring to? How does this compare with your country?

11. Italy is described as the land of romance and love. What would be the attractions of a Latin love affair?

12. Italian children are included from birth in all social activities. What do you see as the advantages and disadvantages of this?

13. Is moving to another country as an adult a courageous act or an escapist fantasy? Would you do it?

14. The book makes many references to Italians as seen from an Anglo point of view. What do you imagine Italians think of Anglos?

Acknowledgements

Grateful thanks to Lyn Tranter and Nikki Davies at Australian Literary Management, Fiona Henderson and Katie Stackhouse at Random House, Jo Jarrah for her editing, and Clare Moss who got me started.

About the Author

Sue Howard was born in London and spent her early years in Australia and England. She has two children, and is currently working as a freelance writer and teacher in Pisa.

More great travel memoirs
from Bantam

Almost French

A New Life in Paris

SARAH TURNBULL

ALICE STEINBACH

WITHOUT
RESERVATIONS

The Travels of an Independent Woman

EDUCATING
ALICE

Adventures of a Curious Woman

ALICE STEINBACH

Bestselling author of *Without Reservations*